RAINBOW magic®

Dazzling Dance Fairies

Collection 1

ORCHARD

The Fairyland Palace
Alexander Willow's House
Wetherbury College
The Village Hall
Wetherbury Train Station
LONDON THIS WAY

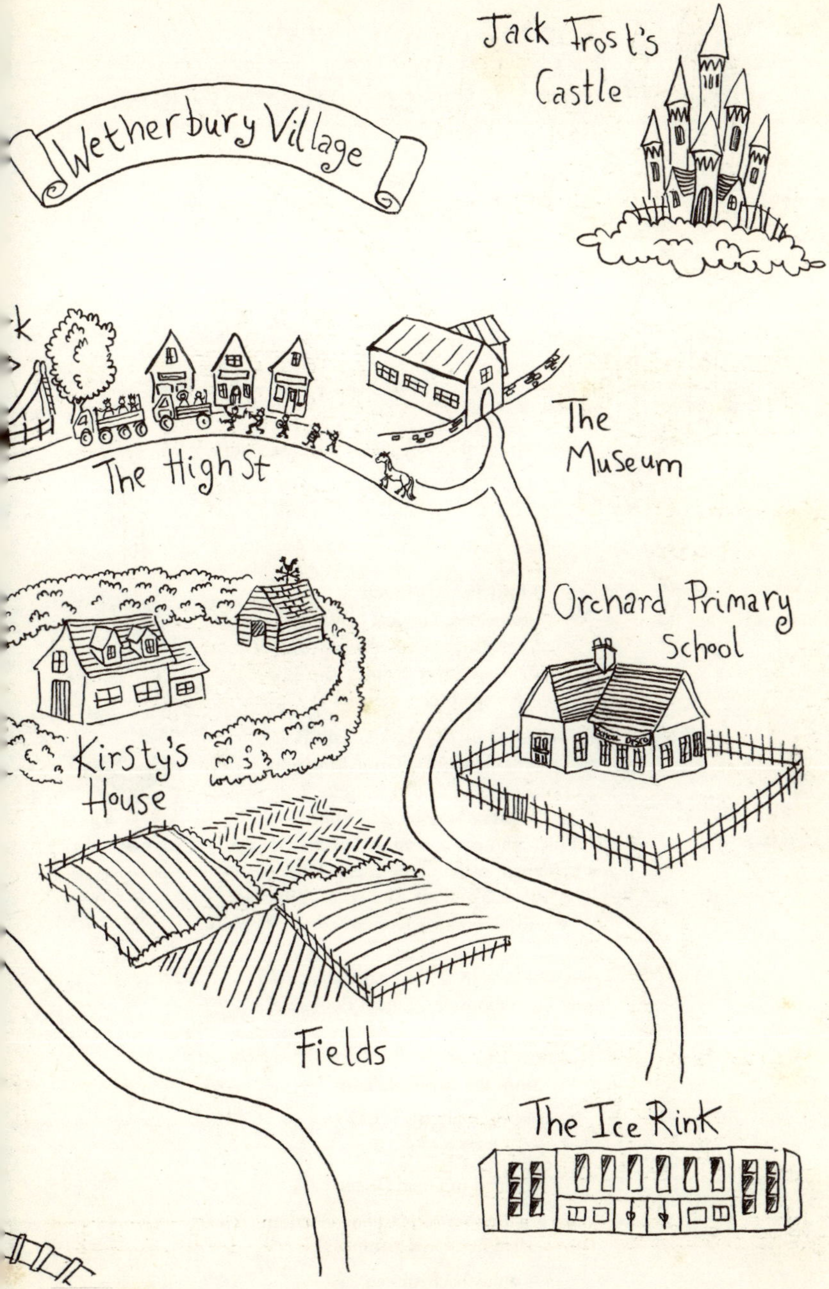
Wetherbury Village
Jack Frost's Castle
The High St
The Museum
Orchard Primary School
Kirsty's House
Fields
The Ice Rink

For my cousin Becky,

who could outwit the goblins every time.

Special thanks to

Narinder Dhami

ORCHARD BOOKS
338 Euston Road, London NW1 3BH
Orchard Books Australia
Level 17/207 Kent Street, Sydney, NSW 2000
A Paperback Original

First published in 2007 by Orchard Books
This collection published in Great Britain in 2013

A CIP catalogue record for this book is available
from the British Library.

ISBN 978 1 40832 941 2
1 3 5 7 9 10 8 6 4 2

Printed in Great Britain

Orchard Books is a division of Hachette Children's Books,
an Hachette UK company

www.hachette.co.uk

Contents

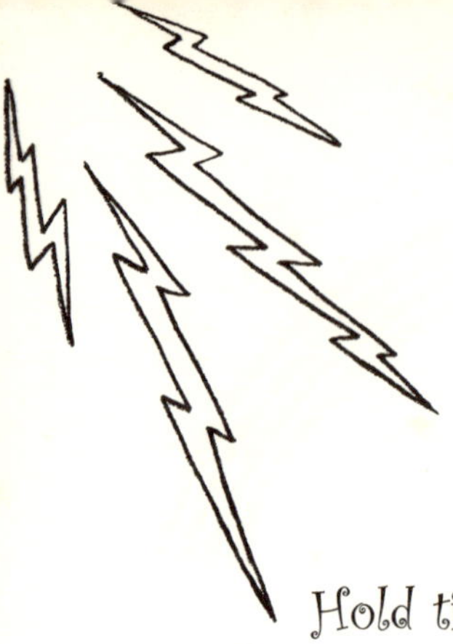

Hold tight to the ribbons, please.
You goblins now may feel a breeze.
I'm summoning a hurricane
To take the ribbons away again.

But, goblins, you'll be swept up too,
For I have work for you to do.
Guard each ribbon carefully,
By using this new power to freeze.

Bethany the Ballet Fairy

by Daisy Meadows

Contents

Fairies in a Whirl

"I'm *really* looking forward to this!" exclaimed Rachel Walker to her best friend, Kirsty Tate. "I *love* ballet."

"Me, too," Kirsty agreed, raising her voice above the noise of the train as it rattled over a bumpy bit of track. "I've never seen *Swan Lake* before."

"I've heard that this is a fantastic

production," Kirsty's mum said. "The scenery is supposed to be gorgeous."

"Well, let's hope it keeps Dad awake!" Kirsty laughed, glancing at her dad who was fast asleep in the corner seat. "I'm so pleased you could come, Rachel. Wasn't it lucky that your school finished for half-term the day before ours? You wouldn't have been here in time to come with us otherwise."

Rachel nodded. Because their families lived quite a long way apart, she was staying with Kirsty for the whole week of the half-term holiday.

"We'll be in London soon," said

Mrs Tate, as the train drew into a station. "This is the last stop before we get there."

Kirsty stared out of the window as the train slowed. Suddenly her attention was caught by a flash of icy blue streaking past the window. Puzzled, Kirsty leaned forward for a closer look.

To her amazement, she saw seven little fairies being tumbled through the air by a tiny icy whirlwind. As Kirsty watched, the fairies landed safely in one of the baskets of flowers suspended from the station roof.

Kirsty and Rachel knew a lot about fairies because the two girls shared an amazing secret. They were best friends with the fairies, and had often helped them to defeat mean Jack Frost and his naughty goblin servants, who were always causing trouble. Now it looked as if their fairy friends might need the girls' help once more.

Almost bursting with excitement, Kirsty glanced at Rachel. But she could see that her friend hadn't noticed anything.

"Mum, I'm feeling hungry," Kirsty said quickly. "Do you think Rachel and I could go and get some biscuits from the buffet car?"

Mrs Tate nodded. "But not too many," she warned. "Remember we're going out for dinner after the show."

Kirsty nodded as she and Rachel got up from their seats.

"Rachel, I've just seen *s*even fairies on the station platform!" Kirsty gasped, as soon as they'd left the carriage.

Rachel looked thrilled. "Seven fairies!" she exclaimed. "Where?"

"Right here!" Kirsty said, pulling down the window that lay directly opposite the basket of fairies. "Hello!" she called softly, hoping the fairies would hear her.

The fairies were dusting themselves off among the pansies, but at the sound of Kirsty's voice, one of them looked up and saw the girls. Her tiny face lit up, and a moment later all seven fairies were zooming over to join Kirsty and Rachel. They flew inside the train and Kirsty shut the window.

"You're Rachel and Kirsty!" declared one of the fairies, happily. "I've seen you with the King and Queen in Fairyland."

The girls smiled at the tiny fairy, who was dressed in a sparkling white tutu and pink ballet shoes.

"I'm so pleased you're here," the fairy went on. "We're the Dance Fairies. I'm Bethany the Ballet Fairy, and this is Jade the Disco Fairy, Rebecca the Rock 'n' Roll Fairy, Tasha the Tap Dance Fairy, Jessica the Jazz Fairy, Saskia the Salsa Fairy and Imogen the Ice Dance Fairy."

Rachel and Kirsty smiled at the fairies, feeling quite dazzled by their gorgeous outfits. The fairies managed to smile back, but the girls could see that their eyes were sad and their sparkling wings drooped.

"Has something gone wrong?" asked Rachel.

Bethany nodded. "It's Jack Frost!" she announced miserably. "He's just cast a spell to throw us out of Fairyland and into the human world. That's why we're here. But, worst of all, he's stolen our magic Dance Ribbons!"

Jack Frost Spells Trouble

"Oh, no!" Rachel exclaimed. "Jack Frost's up to his old tricks again!"

"What exactly do the ribbons do?" asked Kirsty.

"They make sure that all dancing goes well and is fun, both in Fairyland and in the human world," Bethany explained. "But the ribbons will only work properly if they are each attached to the right fairy's wand. If we don't get our ribbons back, nobody will be able to dance properly ever again!"

Rachel and Kirsty stared at each other in horror.

"That's terrible!" Kirsty exclaimed. "Is there anything we can do to help?" Rachel asked.

Bethany smiled gratefully at them. "Thank you, girls!" she cried. "Even though Jack Frost's spell cast us into the human world, a little bit of fairy magic must have helped to bring us here to you! Will you come to Fairyland with us, so that we can tell the King and

Queen what's happened?"

"We'd love to, but what about my mum and dad?" asked Kirsty. "They'll wonder where we are."

"Fairy magic will make sure you return to the human world as if no time has passed," Bethany replied reassuringly.

Rachel and Kirsty grinned and Bethany showered the girls with white and pink glittering fairy dust. As the magical sparkles floated down around them, the girls shrank to fairy-size and translucent wings appeared on their shoulders.

Next moment, the girls were whizzing through the air in a haze of fairy dust, and, in no time at all, they were hovering above the golden Fairyland palace with its four pink turrets.

The King and Queen were strolling in the palace gardens. They looked extremely surprised to see the seven Dance Fairies, as well as Rachel and Kirsty, fluttering towards them.

"Good afternoon, Dance Fairies!"

King Oberon called. "And welcome, Kirsty and Rachel."

"How are you, girls?" asked Queen Titania, smiling kindly at Kirsty and Rachel. "Do you need our help?"

"No, Your Majesty," Rachel replied, shaking her head.

"It's us Dance Fairies who need Kirsty and Rachel's help, Your Majesties!" Bethany declared. "Jack Frost has just stolen our magic Dance Ribbons!"

The King and Queen frowned.

"He sent us all hurtling into the human world too," Bethany went on. "But, luckily, fairy magic led us to Kirsty and Rachel, and then we all came back to Fairyland to tell you what had happened."

"Let's see exactly what went on," said Queen Titania, leading the way to the golden pool in the palace gardens. The Queen waved her wand over the pool and then nodded at Bethany. The Ballet Fairy immediately touched her wand gently to the water and ripples began to spread across its surface.

"As Your Majesties already know, Jack Frost was fed up because whenever he throws a party, none of his goblins can dance properly!" Bethany explained. "So today, Jack Frost asked the other Dance Fairies and me to teach the goblins how to dance."

"We thought it meant that Jack Frost had changed his ways and wanted to be friends with us," Jade the Disco Fairy put in. "But we were wrong!"

Everyone watched as a picture appeared in the pool. Rachel and Kirsty saw the seven Dance Fairies knocking on the door of Jack Frost's ice castle.

"Are those the magic ribbons?" asked Kirsty, pointing at the fairies' wands in the picture. Each fairy had a ribbon trailing from the tip of her wand.

Bethany nodded as the picture changed to show Jack Frost opening the door. His cold, sulky face broke into a smile as he saw the Dance Fairies waiting outside.

"Come in!" he cried, "We're all ready for you!"

Rachel and Kirsty watched as Jack Frost led the Dance Fairies into the throne room. There his goblin servants were lined up, dressed in their finest outfits. They wore outsized hats with large plumed feathers, embroidered waistcoats and velvet trousers. Rachel and Kirsty smiled. They'd never seen the goblins look quite like this before!

Jack Frost sat down on his magnificent ice throne, and watched as the Dance Fairies began the lesson.

The goblins were *terrible* dancers.

They stumbled across the throne room, frequently tripping over their own feet and each other's. Then they started arguing, and their yelling drowned out the beautiful music that the Dance Fairies had conjured up.

But, as Rachel and Kirsty watched, the Dance Fairies quickly began to work their magic. Gradually the goblins stopped bumping into each other and arguing, and began gliding around the room in time to the music instead.

Kirsty nudged Rachel. "Look, even Jack Frost seems to be enjoying himself!" she pointed out.

Jack Frost was sitting on his throne, merrily tapping his foot along to the music. But, suddenly, he jumped up from his seat, a spiteful smile on his face.

"NOW!" he bellowed.

Immediately the goblins dashed forward and grabbed all seven ribbons from the Dance Fairies' wands. Whooping with glee, they then began waving the ribbons triumphantly in the air.

The fairies were taken completely by surprise, but they quickly raised their wands to cast a spell.

Unfortunately, they were too late. Jack Frost was already pointing his wand at them, and shouting a spell of his own. "Come, freezing wind and ice and snow. To the human world, Dance Fairies, GO!"

Instantly, an icy wind whistled through the throne room. Rachel and Kirsty watched in horror as the Dance Fairies were swept up in the freezing whirlwind and carried out of the window.

"So *that's* how we ended up in the human world!" Bethany sighed, as the images in the pool faded. "And that's how Jack Frost got our ribbons!"

Ribbons Whisked Away

"We *must* get the ribbons back," King Oberon declared.

"We'll all go to Jack Frost's ice castle immediately!" Queen Titania decided.

She waved her wand and Kirsty and Rachel heard a bell tinkling in the distance. A few moments later there was the sound of hooves, and a carriage made of shining crystal drew up outside the palace gates. The carriage was drawn by six unicorns with gleaming white coats and crystal horns. They came to a halt, tossing their snowy manes and neighing softly.

"Look, it's Bertram!" Rachel pointed out as the King and Queen led them over to the carriage.

Bertram, the frog footman, was sitting at the front of the carriage. He gave the girls a cheery wave.

Kirsty and Rachel climbed in and sat down next to the King and Queen on pink velvet cushions. Meanwhile the Dance Fairies perched on the unicorns' backs, and the carriage set off through Fairyland.

It wasn't long before they'd left the beautiful green meadows behind. Rachel and Kirsty shivered as the temperature began to fall.

"There's Jack Frost's ice castle," Rachel said. The girls had visited the castle before, but it was still very scary-looking. It stood on a tall hill under a gloomy sky, and it was built of sheets of ice with towers topped by icy blue turrets.

"And there's Jack Frost!" Kirsty added, as a head poked out of one of the windows.

Jack Frost scowled when he saw the carriage approaching, and ducked back inside the castle again.

"Somehow, I don't think he wants to return the magic ribbons!" Rachel remarked.

The carriage drew up beside the castle and Bertram hopped down to help everyone out. But, as they made their way towards the heavy castle door, it was suddenly flung open and Jack Frost stalked out.

"You're too late!" he snapped. "The ribbons are gone, and there's nothing you can do about it!"

A great shriek above their heads made

Rachel, Kirsty and all the fairies glance upwards. They saw a goblin fly out of one of the castle windows, carried along by a huge whirlwind. He was clutching a pink ribbon which flapped in the breeze.

"That's my magic ribbon!" Bethany cried. She tried to fly towards the shrieking goblin, but the icy whirlwind pushed her back. In fact, the wind was so strong that Rachel, Kirsty and the others could hardly keep their feet on the ground.

"There's more of them!" Rachel shouted, pointing upwards.

Six more goblins were tumbling through the air. Each of them holding on to a different ribbon.

"I command you to return the magic ribbons, Jack Frost!" King Oberon cried. Battling against the wind, the King lifted his wand and murmured some magic words. Immediately, the wind dropped, but the goblins had already vanished. Rachel and Kirsty glanced at each other in dismay.

"You're coming with us, Jack Frost!" King Oberon said sternly. "And you'll stay under guard at our palace until all the ribbons are returned to the Dance Fairies."

"Oh, but you'll *never* get the ribbons back!" Jack Frost cackled. "I've told my goblin servants to hide in the human world, and there they'll stay! And besides..." he added, pausing and looking even more sly than usual. "Even if the fairies *do* find my goblins, they'll soon see that this time there's more to them than meets the eye!"

And he laughed even louder.

King Oberon sighed and waved his wand again. A swirl of fairy dust lifted Jack Frost off his feet and swept him into the royal carriage.

The doors slammed shut and Jack Frost's smile vanished.

"Girls, the goblins are hiding with the Dance Ribbons in the human world!" said Queen Titania, turning to Rachel and Kirsty. "Will you help the Dance Fairies to find them and get them back?

Rachel and Kirsty nodded solemnly.

"Each ribbon is attracted to its own type of dance," Bethany explained, "so each ribbon's magic will draw the goblin towards places where that ribbon's style of dance is taking place."

"Oh!" Rachel exclaimed. "We're going to the ballet tonight. Maybe the goblin with the Ballet Ribbon will be there!"

Bethany looked very excited. "I'll come with you, just in case!" she said.

Queen Titania was already lifting her wand to shower them with magic. "Good luck!" she called.

Looking more hopeful, the other Dance Fairies waved farewell, as Queen Titania's magic whisked Bethany, Rachel and Kirsty away. A moment later they were back on the train.

"We'd better go and buy some biscuits or Mum will wonder why we're back empty-handed!" Kirsty said, as Bethany hid in Rachel's pocket.

"We're almost there, girls," Mrs Tate said when Kirsty and Rachel arrived back from the buffet car. Mr Tate had woken up and they were gathering their things together.

Outside the station they took a cab to the ballet. As they went inside the theatre and took their seats, Rachel and Kirsty were amazed to see how beautiful it was. There were sweeping gold balconies, a domed roof painted with ballet scenes, and golden chairs with plush red cushions.

"Are you OK, Bethany?" Rachel whispered as the lights began to dim. Immediately the fairy peeped out of Rachel's pocket and smiled.

The curtain rose, and Kirsty and Rachel gasped as they gazed at the wintry scene before them. A huge frozen lake surrounded by leafless trees covered most of the stage, and a full moon hung in the sky. Everything was covered with frost which sparkled under the bright stage lights. Dancers in feathery white tutus were poised, motionless, here and there.

"It's lovely!" Rachel breathed, and Kirsty nodded.

They waited breathlessly for the ballet to begin, but none of the dancers moved a muscle. Puzzled, Rachel and Kirsty glanced at each other as the spectators began murmuring in confusion.

"Why is nobody dancing?" whispered Mrs Tate.

"This is all very strange!" Mr Tate added.

"Something's not right," Bethany whispered to Rachel and Kirsty. "And I'm sure it has something to do with Jack Frost's goblins!"

Frozen!

Still the dancers didn't move. The curtain fell, and the mutterings of the audience grew louder.

"We must try to save the ballet!" Bethany said urgently.

Rachel nodded. "We need to find that goblin!" she said.

"Dad, can we go and get

a programme?" Kirsty asked quickly.

Mr Tate nodded. "Don't be long though," he said. "I'm sure the ballet will start again soon."

"We should start backstage," Bethany told the girls as they hurried out into the lobby.

"But we'll need to make sure that we're not seen," Kirsty pointed out anxiously.

They ran to the back of the theatre and cautiously Rachel pushed open the stage door. A doorman sat in a little booth just inside the entrance.

"He's not moving," Kirsty whispered.

"And look!" Rachel added, as they went further backstage. "Neither is anyone else!"

All around them were stagehands who had been moving scenery, and dancers who had been warming up. But every single person was now completely frozen in place.

"They're as cold as ice!" Kirsty said, touching one of the dancer's arms. "Maybe Jack Frost has given his goblins a wand of ice magic."

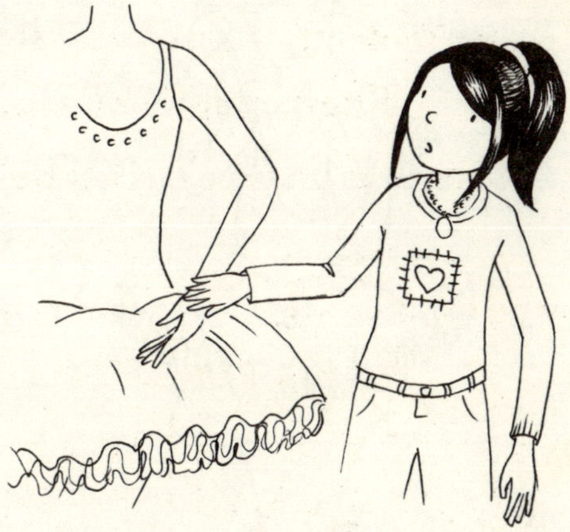

"Listen!" said Bethany suddenly, "I can hear someone giggling!"

"It's coming from the other side of the stage," Rachel said.

Quickly the friends hurried across the curtained stage, weaving their way in and out of the motionless dancers. As they neared the other side, they saw a very strange sight.

A goblin wearing pink tights was struggling to get into a fluffy white tutu. He had jammed a pair of dainty white ballet shoes onto his feet, and around his head he had tied Bethany's pink Ballet Ribbon – larger now that it was in the

human world – in a neat bow.

Rachel and Kirsty put their hands over their mouths to muffle their giggles.

"I thought the goblins were supposed to be hiding," Kirsty whispered. "This one isn't doing a very good job of it!"

"The magic of the ribbons is so strong that anyone who has one can't help but dance!" Bethany explained, fluttering out of Rachel's pocket. "Come on, let's get my ribbon back!"

The goblin was so busy trying to squeeze into the tutu, he didn't notice Bethany and the girls until they were right in front of him. Kirsty was glad to see that he didn't seem to have a magic wand, either.

"Give my magic ribbon back, please!" Bethany said firmly.

The goblin scowled at her. "Go away, pesky fairy!" he muttered. "I'm not giving the ribbon back! I like being good at dancing. And, even better, I'm ruining the ballet for everyone else! Jack Frost is going to be *very* pleased with me."

"That's mean," Kirsty said.

The goblin looked thoughtful. Then suddenly he smiled sweetly at Kirsty. "Well, OK," he said. "You can take the ribbon, but you'll have to untie it for me. I did it up too tightly."

Rachel frowned, feeling suspicious. Why was the goblin being so nice all of a sudden?

"Kirsty, don't—" Rachel began. But she was too late. Kirsty had already stepped forward to undo the ribbon. And as she did so, the goblin touched her wrist and said, "Freeze!"

Instantly, poor Kirsty was frozen stiff.

Mooning Around

The goblin roared with laughter.

"Oh, no!" Rachel gasped, staring in horror at her frozen friend.

"Jack Frost must have given the goblins freezing powers," Bethany guessed. "So that's what he meant when he said there was more to the goblins than meets the eye!"

The goblin stepped forward, and reached out a big green hand towards Rachel.

"Oh, no, you don't!" Bethany cried, waving her wand over Rachel, and transforming her instantly into a tiny fairy. Rachel zoomed away from the goblin's touch and joined Bethany, out of his reach.

"Teehee!" the goblin chuckled. "You can't touch me, or I'll freeze you too!" And still laughing, he ran onto the stage.

"What are we going to do about Kirsty?" Rachel asked anxiously as she and Bethany flew after him.

"Don't worry, Rachel," Bethany said,

as they perched in one of the cardboard trees. "The spell will wear off soon and Kirsty will be fine."

Below them on the stage the goblin had begun to dance. Rachel's eyes widened as he performed perfect jetés, pirouettes and arabesques.

"He's a brilliant dancer!" she said.

"It's only because he's got my magic ribbon," Bethany sniffed. "We must get it back!"

Rachel watched the goblin moving around the stage and in and out of the wings. He was touching all the ballerinas and stagehands as he went past them, and Rachel guessed he was making sure they all remained frozen.

Suddenly Rachel noticed the large, pale moon, made out of tissue paper,

hanging from the top of the stage. It was suspended in the air from a rope, and as she looked at it, an idea popped into her head.

"Bethany," she whispered, "if the goblin was underneath the paper moon, we could drop it down on him and grab the ribbon!"

"Great idea, Rachel!" Bethany agreed eagerly. "It's very light, so it won't hurt him. But how will we get the goblin to stand underneath it?"

Rachel frowned. But before she could suggest anything, she saw Kirsty hurry onto the stage below. Kirsty was keeping a close eye on the dancing goblin, but she was also looking around for Rachel and Bethany.

"The freezing spell's worn off and Kirsty's looking for us!" Rachel whispered to Bethany. "Maybe she can help us get the goblin underneath the moon."

Bethany nodded. "We'll have to be careful though," she whispered back. "We don't want the goblin to guess what we're up to!"

The little fairy waved her wand and a few magic sparkles drifted downwards, making Kirsty look up and spot her friends in the tree.

Rachel immediately pointed at the moon and then at the goblin, trying to explain to Kirsty that they needed him to be underneath the moon.

Rachel could see her friend frowning in concentration as she watched, but would she understand what Rachel wanted her to do?

Ballet Back on Track

For a moment Kirsty looked puzzled. Then she nodded and turned away. "I want that ribbon," she called to the goblin. "And don't even *think* of trying to freeze me again!"

The goblin scowled at her. "I can freeze you any time I want!" he snapped back.

"I don't think so!" Kirsty said mockingly.

Rachel and Bethany watched hopefully as Kirsty casually moved closer to the moon.

"I'll show you!" the goblin chuckled, skipping gleefully towards her.

Just a few more steps! Rachel thought, holding her breath. Kirsty moved away a little and the goblin followed, his hand outstretched to freeze her. Now he was right underneath the paper moon. With a flick of her wrist Bethany sent a burst of fairy sparkles towards the rope which held the moon up.

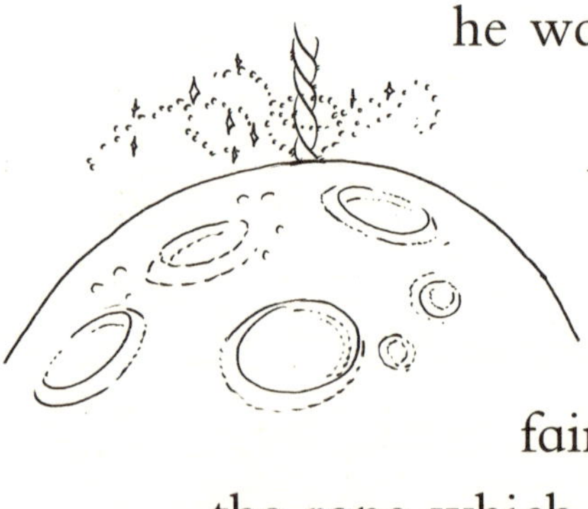

The rope immediately untied itself and the moon plummeted, knocking the goblin to the floor.

"Agghh!" the goblin yelled in surprise.

Quick as a flash, Kirsty whipped the magic ribbon from the goblin's head. He sat up, looking furious but unhurt.

She tried to jump aside as the goblin grabbed at her wrist but she wasn't quick enough. Rachel's heart skipped a beat as the goblin shouted, "Freeze!" once more.

But, this time, nothing happened!

Kirsty looked relieved and waved up at her friends. "I'm fine!" she called. Bethany and Rachel flew down to join her.

"It looks like Jack Frost only gave you the freezing power while you had the ribbon," Bethany told the goblin with a grin.

Looking extremely sulky, the goblin

stuck his tongue out at her. "Well, we still have the other magic ribbons!" he snapped. "And I'll make sure we hang onto them!" Scowling, he jumped up and ran off.

"Thank you so much, girls!" Bethany said joyfully. She sent a stream of magic fairy dust towards the ribbon in Kirsty's hand and it floated over to the little fairy, shrinking down to its usual Fairyland size as it did so. As the girls watched,

the ribbon reattached itself to Bethany's wand in a cloud of pink sparkles, shining an even deeper pink colour as it did so.

"Now, hurry back to your seats while I put everything right here on stage," Bethany told Rachel and Kirsty. "Everyone will be unfreezing soon, and the performance will begin. Thankfully, now that I have my ribbon back, it should go perfectly!"

"Goodbye!" Rachel and Kirsty called to the fairy, hurrying towards the stage door. As they went, they saw the dancers and stagehands beginning to unfreeze.

"Let's get this show on the road!" one of the stagehands declared.

Rachel and Kirsty grinned at each other. Then they quickly bought a programme and dashed back to their seats.

"Just in time, girls!" whispered Mr Tate as they sat down. "The ballet's starting now."

Rachel and Kirsty gazed eagerly at the beautiful scene on the stage once more.

The paper moon was back in its proper place again, and seated on top of it was Bethany. Rachel and Kirsty smiled as the little fairy waved at them before vanishing in a puff of silvery-white sparkles.

"This is going to be great!" Rachel sighed happily as the dancers began to pirouette across the frozen lake on stage. "But we can't forget that we've got six more magic ribbons to find."

"Yes, and we'll have to be careful of the goblins' new freezing powers," Kirsty whispered. "Still, I can't wait for our next fairy adventure!"

Jade the Disco Fairy

by Daisy Meadows

Contents

Girls Go Dancing

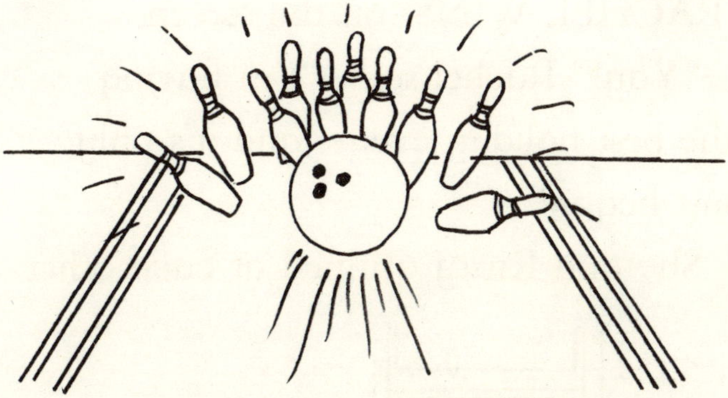

"Strike!" cheered Kirsty Tate, as Rachel's ball sent all ten pins flying at the end of the bowling lane.

"Hurrah!" Rachel cried in delight.

"That's your third strike of the game!" Kirsty's dad said, smiling. "Well done, Rachel."

"And it looks like you won the game,

too!" Mrs Tate added, gazing up at the electronic scoreboard in front of her.

The girls went to see. Sure enough, flashing green letters spelled out 'RACHEL WINS' on the screen.

"Yay!" Rachel said. "I'm having the best holiday ever – and it's only just begun!"

She and Kirsty grinned at each other.

Rachel was staying with Kirsty's family for the autumn half-term holiday, and the two girls always had very exciting adventures whenever they were together. *Fairy* adventures! This time was no different. Only yesterday, they'd met the seven Dance Fairies, who'd asked for their help. The girls had said yes straightaway. They loved helping the fairies!

"Well, girls," Mr Tate said as the scoreboard flashed 'GAME OVER'. "It's time to take off your bowling shoes, and put on your dancing shoes. It's the school disco this evening, remember?"

"I can't wait," Kirsty said eagerly. "Rachel and I love dancing, don't we?"

Rachel nodded, knowing Kirsty was thinking about the Dance Fairies. "Definitely," she replied. "Come on, let's go!"

Once they were back at the Tates' house, the girls got changed for the disco in Kirsty's bedroom. Rachel was wearing a pretty purple party dress, and Kirsty picked out a pink sparkly top and a pair of black trousers.

"I can't wait to see all your friends again," Rachel said, brushing her hair in front of the mirror.

"I really enjoyed meeting them at your birthday party. It'll be great to dance with them tonight."

Kirsty went over to check that her door was closed properly. "We might even get to see another of the Dance Fairies too!" she added in a low voice.

"I hope so," Rachel said eagerly. Yesterday, she and Kirsty had met all seven Dance Fairies and been magically whisked away to Fairyland, where they'd learned that the Dance Fairies' magical ribbons had been stolen by the bad fairy, Jack Frost.

The fairies had explained that the magic ribbons made sure that dancing went smoothly and was fun, for everyone in Fairyland as well as in the human world. Jack Frost had stolen the ribbons because he wanted his goblins to be able to dance well at a party he was throwing.

Rachel and Kirsty, together with the Dance Fairies and the Fairy King and Queen, had gone to Jack Frost's ice castle to try and get the ribbons back.

But, when he saw them coming, sneaky Jack Frost had sent all the ribbons into the human world, along with a goblin to guard each one.

Yesterday, the girls had helped Bethany the Ballet Fairy find the goblin with her Ballet Ribbon, and they'd got the ribbon safely back, but they'd been shocked to discover that Jack Frost had given his goblin servants a new magical power. While they had the ribbons, the goblins could freeze anything they wanted with their master's icy magic!

Kirsty picked up a hair-clip and began fastening it in her hair. Then she stopped and looked at Rachel with a worried expression. "I've just had a thought," she said. "What if the school disco is ruined because the Disco Ribbon is still missing?"

Rachel bit her lip. "I hope it's not," she said. "It would be awful if the school dance was spoilt. We'll have to look out for the goblin, and hope that we can get the magic ribbon back to Jade the Disco Fairy before anything goes wrong."

Kirsty nodded. "I don't like the thought of meeting another goblin who can freeze us," she shivered, "but we've got to try and save the disco!"

Groovy Goblin

"See you later, girls," Mrs Tate said, as she dropped Kirsty and Rachel off at the school hall that evening. "Have fun!"

"Bye Mum, we will," Kirsty replied, waving. She and Rachel walked towards the doors. They could hear music pounding as they approached and exchanged hopeful looks.

"The disco seems to be going all right so far," Rachel said optimistically. "I mean, the music's playing, so it hasn't been cancelled or anything..."

Kirsty pushed open the doors. "Oh, and look!" she cried happily, "The hall is never usually this pretty!"

Rachel and Kirsty

gazed around the large school hall. Balloons and streamers were pinned in the top corners of the room and coloured lights flashed on the dance floor. Above their heads, sparkling glitter balls hung from the ceiling, sending tiny colourful reflections spinning all around the room.

"Wow!" said Rachel.

"It looks great, but no one is dancing."

The girls looked at the empty dance floor. There were clusters of girls and boys all around the room, but nobody was actually dancing to the music.

"Maybe it's a good thing," Kirsty said in a low voice. "While the Disco Ribbon isn't on Jade's wand, everyone's dancing would probably be really bad anyway."

Rachel was just about to agree when the song changed and two adults took to the dance floor, with rather self-conscious smiles on their faces.

Kirsty's eyes widened. "It's Mr Collins and Mrs Adams!" she said.

"It looks like they're trying to get the disco started," Rachel added, watching as the teachers began to dance. Mr Collins started shaking his hips to the music, but somehow this caused his legs to go in opposite directions and he slipped on the floor and went flying into Mrs Adams. Mrs Adams wobbled as he crashed into her, and her arms flailed as she tried to keep her balance.

Kirsty looked at Rachel. "Oh, no," she said. "I was afraid this would happen!"

Rachel nodded. "We really need the Disco Ribbon!"

People around the room were giggling because the two teachers seemed to be getting worse by the second. Mrs Adams trod on Mr Collins' toes, then he knocked her glasses off as he attempted to do a groovy finger-pointing movement!

"They are so bad," a girl standing near Kirsty and Rachel giggled to her friends. "I can't believe they're such awful dancers!"

"Come on, we can't be any worse than them," one of her friends replied. "Let's go and show them how it's done!"

The group of girls edged onto the dance floor and started dancing, keeping a safe distance from the floundering teachers. Then another few girls joined them, followed by some boys. It seemed that

the teachers' awful dancing had given everyone else a bit of confidence. In just a few minutes, the empty dance floor was packed.

"Shall we dance too?" Rachel asked, turning to Kirsty.

But Kirsty was staring at the dancers, looking alarmed. "It's getting a bit dangerous out there, if you ask me!" she replied. "Look!"

Rachel turned back to see that it wasn't just the teachers who were dancing badly now. *Nobody* seemed able to dance well at all! As Rachel watched in horror, she saw one girl lose her balance and crash into her friend. Then, on the other side of the room, she saw a boy fall over, dragging a couple of mates down with him.

"I've never seen such awful dancing," Rachel whispered to Kirsty in dismay. "Someone's going to get hurt in a minute!"

Kirsty nodded. "We really must find the ribbon," she whispered back, "before this turns into a disaster! Come on, let's start looking."

Rachel scanned the room, wondering where they should begin their search, when her gaze fell upon a dancer in the far corner. He was rather short and dressed in white flared trousers and high platform shoes. A huge pair of sunglasses hid most of his face. "Ooh," she said to Kirsty, pointing the dancer out. "*He's* a good dancer, isn't he?"

Kirsty looked at the boy. "Yes, he is," she agreed. "How strange that he's such a funky dancer, when everyone else is so terrible."

Rachel frowned thoughtfully. "Actually, the people who are dancing near him aren't that bad either," she said.

The girls stared at the boy as he whirled about the dance floor.

"I don't recognise him," Kirsty said after a moment or two. "I'm sure I haven't seen him at school before. I wonder if he's someone's little brother?"

Just then, the song finished and the girls edged forward, keen to get a better look at the dancing boy as he came to a stop.

Kirsty frowned as she spotted that he had unusually pointy ears, and even though the flashing disco lights were making everyone's faces turn funny colours, she was sure she could see a greenish tinge to his skin...

"Rachel!" Kirsty gulped. "I think that boy is really a *goblin*! Look at his ears!"

Rachel peered across the dance floor. "You're right!" she exclaimed. "He must be the goblin with the Disco Ribbon! *That*'s why he's such a good dancer."

Kirsty nodded, her eyes fixed on the goblin who was now dancing to the next song, wiggling to the beat on his gigantic platform shoes. "And that's why everyone near him is dancing well," she added. "The Disco Ribbon's magic is affecting them, too!"

"Let's try and get closer," Rachel suggested, "and see if we can spot the magic ribbon."

Kirsty agreed. "Yes," she said. "We might even be able to grab it without him noticing, once we know where it is. He's totally wrapped up in the music."

The girls made their way across the dance floor, dodging the rather erratic dancing that was going on around them. Things weren't made any easier by the fact that there was now quite a crowd around the goblin, all trying to copy his disco moves.

"I thought Jack Frost told his goblins that they had to stay *hidden* with the ribbons," Kirsty said to Rachel over the thump of the music.

"He certainly isn't hiding," Rachel laughed. "But he is in disguise," she added, swerving to avoid a boy who had just managed to trip over his own feet. "Ow!" she gasped suddenly, as somebody else barged right into her, knocking her to the floor.

Kirsty bent down to help her friend up. It was only when the girls were both standing again that they realised something terrible had happened: the goblin had vanished!

Goblin Goes Missing

"Oh, no!" said Rachel, looking around frantically. "Where is he?"

"I can't see him anywhere," Kirsty replied, "but look, the people who were near him are dancing badly now, just like everyone else. He must have gone."

Rachel, who was still staring around, suddenly spotted something rather strange. "Hey," she said. "Look at that glitter ball up there, Kirsty. Is it my imagination or is it shimmering more brightly than the others?"

She and Kirsty gazed up at the glitter ball – and then jumped with surprise as a tiny fairy darted out from behind it in a cloud of green sparkles.

"It's Jade the Disco Fairy!" Kirsty cried. "Thank goodness!"

The girls shielded their eyes from the bright lights as Jade waved at them, and then fluttered down to land on Kirsty's shoulder. Luckily, everyone else was so busy dancing badly and bumping into one another that they didn't notice a tiny fairy joining the disco!

Jade had long blonde hair. She wore a jade-green, halter-neck top, and trousers with a green, swirly print on them. On her feet she wore pretty, high-heeled green sandals.

"Hello, Jade," Rachel said as they moved to the side of the dance floor where it was a little quieter. "Did you see the goblin?"

"I certainly did," Jade said, rolling her eyes. "And I've never seen such a terrible outfit! It's enough to give disco a bad name! Those shoes – I mean, really!"

Kirsty laughed. "Did you see where he went?" she asked. "We lost him."

Jade shook her head. "I lost track of him too," she replied, "but he won't have gone far. If he's got my ribbon, I can guarantee that all he'll want to do is dance! He's bound to stay near the music."

"Well, he's not in the hall any more," Rachel said. "But maybe he's close by."

"Let's go out into the corridor," Kirsty suggested, walking towards a door nearby. "We can start looking there."

The girls and Jade went out of the hall. It was cooler and quieter in the corridor, although they could still hear the music from the disco quite clearly. They hurried along the corridor, peeping into the classrooms they passed.

The first two rooms were empty, but as Kirsty popped her head around the door of the third, she smiled to see the goblin dancing on top of the desks and singing really badly to the disco music.

She drew her head back quickly before he spotted her. "He's in there!" she hissed to Rachel and Jade. "What shall we do?"

"Do?" Jade replied. "We'll go straight in there and ask for my ribbon back, that's what we'll do! Come on!"

Ribbon In Reach

Jade zipped into the classroom, with Rachel and Kirsty right behind her. The goblin was now dancing away on a desk, which lay directly under a solar system mobile that dangled from the ceiling. He was having a great time, boogieing along to the music, his big high shoes banging loudly on the desk top with every step.

Jade fluttered over to him, and the girls gathered by his desk.

"I believe you've got my Disco Ribbon," Jade said. "And I'd like it back now, thank you very much!"

At her words, the goblin pushed his huge sunglasses off his face and almost fell off the desk in surprise to see Jade, Kirsty and Rachel in front of him.

"Go away! Can't you see I'm dancing?" he asked rudely, flicking his sunglasses down onto his nose again, and turning his back on the three friends.

Rachel watched him strutting his stuff. "I hate to say this, but he's actually quite good," she said in a low voice.

"I can't believe he can dance like that in those huge platforms!" Kirsty agreed.

Jade didn't look so impressed. "Hmmmph!" she sniffed crossly. "It's nothing to do with him. It's my ribbon's magic that's making him dance well, that's all."

The goblin danced around, clapping his hands in time to the music and wiggling his bottom.

As he came around to face the girls again, he looked annoyed to see that they were still there. Then a sly smirk appeared on his face. "Hey, why don't you come and join me?" he suggested. "I could teach you my disco routine!"

Kirsty and Rachel shook their heads, backing away warily.

"No chance," Rachel replied. "We know you just want to freeze us!"

"And we're not going to fall for any of your tricks," Kirsty told him.

The goblin gave a cackle. "Well, you're not getting this ribbon back!" he said, pulling a length of sparkly

green out of his pocket. "Maybe I'll freeze you anyway, just for the fun of it!"

He made a leap towards the girls, but Jade quickly waved her wand and turned them into fairies, so that they could zoom out of his way.

Kirsty grinned as she flapped her delicate wings and fluttered out of the goblin's reach. Being able to fly was such fun – and very useful!

The three fairies circled the goblin's head as he glared at them. "Push off!" he growled, climbing back on to his table. "Can't a goblin dance in peace if he wants to?"

"Not with my ribbon, he can't," Jade retorted. "Now hand it over, or we'll buzz around your head like annoying mosquitoes until you do!"

"Then I'll have to *swat* you like mosquitoes!" snarled the goblin, making another leap for them. He held his big hands flat like fly-swatters, and as he did so, the sparkly green Disco Ribbon flew out from between his fingers and looped around the model of Saturn on the solar system mobile above his head.

The goblin looked up and tugged at it, but the ribbon had got caught in Saturn's rings and wouldn't budge. "Stupid thing!" the goblin moaned, jumping up and down and yanking at it with all his might.

The solar system mobile swung dizzily, but the ribbon held fast.

Jade's eyes lit up. "This could be a chance to get my ribbon back!" she said to Rachel and Kirsty in a low voice. "How can we get the goblin to let go of the other end?"

Kirsty grinned. "Tickle him!" she suggested. She and Rachel had discovered on previous fairy adventures that the goblins were *extremely ticklish.*

Jade chuckled. "That's a brilliant idea," she said. "I'll tickle the goblin with my wand, and maybe you two could fly to the mobile and untangle the ribbon while he's distracted."

"Let's do it!" Rachel said eagerly. Jade murmured some magic words and her wand suddenly grew much longer and sprouted a super-tickly, feathery tip! "There," she said with a smile. "Let's see if this does the trick."

She flew down towards the goblin and dusted the feathery wand under his arm while he was reaching up to pull on the ribbon. He immediately shrieked with laughter and lowered his arm. "Ooh! Ooh! Stop it!" he yelped, still holding onto the ribbon and making the planets on the mobile clash together above his head.

Jade didn't stop. She wiggled the wand under his chin next, and the goblin collapsed in giggles.

"Ooh, no! No!" he chortled. "Stop!"

But the little fairy was a blur, flying all around the goblin, tickling him at the backs of his knees and behind his big ears until he was helpless with laughter. The girls watched as the goblin's grip on the ribbon began to slip.

Kirsty and Rachel flew up to the mobile and began trying to untangle the ribbon from Saturn's rings. By now, the goblin was laughing uncontrollably and his sunglasses flew off because his whole body was shaking with giggles. The goblin dropped to his knees, squirming and laughing, and then, to the girls' delight, he dropped the end of the Disco Ribbon.

Bowled Over

"It worked!" Kirsty hissed excitedly, gazing at the dangling ribbon. "Quick, Rachel, we just have to untie this end and we'll have got it!"

"There!" Rachel cried, as the tangled end of the ribbon came free. She reached out to grab it, but before she could get a proper grip, the ribbon slipped straight through her fingers and fell onto the goblin's head!

"Oh, no!" Rachel cried, swooping down to try and retrieve the ribbon.

The goblin, feeling the soft ribbon land on his head, was so surprised that he stopped laughing. Then he realised what had happened and reached up to grab the ribbon. With a look of jubilation on his face, he stuffed it into his trouser pocket and jumped down from the desk. "Can't catch me!" he yelled, and then, sticking his tongue out rudely at the three girls,

he ran straight out of the classroom.

Jade shook her wand, turning it back to normal at once. "After him!" she cried.

Jade, Kirsty and Rachel flapped their wings hard, zoomed across the classroom and soared back into the corridor, after the goblin.

The goblin seemed to be finding it hard to run on his platform shoes, Kirsty noticed. He was very wobbly, and stumbled a few times, although he still managed to keep ahead of the girls.

"Why is he so wobbly on his feet?"

Kirsty asked Jade. "I thought the ribbon helped him keep his balance even with those massive shoes."

"It does," Jade replied, "Just as long as he's disco dancing." She grinned. "But now that he's running instead of dancing, the ribbon's magic doesn't help."

Rachel, Kirsty and Jade flapped their wings even harder, but they

didn't seem able to gain on the goblin.

"We mustn't let him get away!" Rachel cried.

The goblin ran past a door that led into the disco hall, and the three fairies raced after him. As they passed the open door, Kirsty's eye was caught by one of the sparkly glitter balls hanging from the ceiling inside – and then a brilliant idea popped into her head!

"Jade," she called quickly, "do you think you could conjure up a big glitter ball like the ones in the hall?"

Jade frowned. "Yes, of course," she said. "But why?"

"There's no time to explain," Kirsty said, "but could you just magic one up, please, and turn Rachel and me back into girls, too?"

"Sure," Jade replied, looking puzzled. She stopped flying and waved her wand over Kirsty and Rachel. With a flurry of green sparkles, the girls' wings disappeared from their backs, and they were normal girls again.

Jade waved her wand a second time and a stream of green fairy dust swirled from its tip towards Kirsty. Instantly a sparkly green glitter ball appeared in Kirsty's arms.

"He's getting away!" Rachel called urgently, as the goblin got nearer to the end of the corridor.

"Yes, but not for long if you can bowl another strike!" Kirsty said, shoving the glitter ball into Rachel's hands. "Go on, Rachel! Bowl that goblin over!"

Rachel laughed as she realised what Kirsty had in mind. "I'll do my best," she said, bending down. Her eye firmly fixed on the running goblin, she took careful aim and bowled the glitter ball.

*Wh*oosh! Along the corridor it rolled, perfectly straight, heading directly for the goblin. *CRASH!* It whacked right into the goblin's platform shoes, sending him flying!

"STRIKE!" Rachel, Kirsty and Jade cheered in the same breath, hurrying down the corridor to where the goblin lay sprawled on the floor.

"Great bowling, Rachel!" Jade declared.

"Thanks," Rachel said, with a grin. "Now where's the Disco Ribbon?"

As the girls arrived, the goblin was desperately trying to get to his feet. But he couldn't quite regain his balance and his arms flailed wildly as he tried to stand up on his huge platform shoes.

Thump! Down he went again, and, this time, the ribbon spilled out of his pocket. Kirsty quickly darted forward and snatched it up before the goblin could even *think* about using freezing magic on her.

"Thanks Mr Goblin," she said, dodging smartly out of the goblin's way.

The goblin kicked off his platform shoes in a rage and got to his feet, rubbing his bottom where he'd bumped down on it and glowering at the girls.

"Stupid shoes! I'd have got away if it hadn't been for *them*!" he complained, and then he stomped off without another word, his big green feet slapping along the floor.

"Here you are, Jade," Kirsty said proudly, holding the Disco Ribbon up for the little fairy.

Jade waved her wand and green sparkles swirled all over the ribbon, making it shrink back to its Fairyland size.

"Thank you, girls," Jade said, smiling as she reattached the ribbon to the end

of her wand. A burst of sparkles surrounded the wand and the ribbon as they came together, and the ribbon seemed to glow an even deeper green.

"That's more like it," Jade said, twirling her wand with a smile on her face. "Disco divas everywhere will move and groove a whole lot better now!"

"Great," Rachel said, beaming. "No more treading on toes at the school disco, then, I hope!"

Jade shook her head. "Definitely not," she replied. "Go and have a look, you'll see that everyone is having a much better time in the hall now."

"Hurrah!" Kirsty said, and then she strained to listen as a new song started up in the disco. "Oh, I love this one!" she exclaimed, doing a little dance on the spot. "Even the music seems better now, Jade!"

Jade grinned and kissed both girls. "Thanks again," she said. "Now go and have some fun. I can see Kirsty's dying to be a disco diva herself!"

"I'll do my best," Kirsty laughed. "Bye, Jade!"

"Bye," Rachel added, waving at the fairy. "Come on, Kirsty, let's hit the dance floor!"

Jade fluttered away down the corridor, leaving a trail of green sparkles in her wake, and Kirsty and Rachel boogied their way back into the school hall. Sure enough, the dance floor was full, and everyone was having fun. But, best of all, nobody was falling over or bumping into each other any more.

The two friends made their way onto the packed dance floor and joined in the dancing.

"I'm so glad we helped find the Disco Ribbon," Rachel called over to Kirsty with a grin. "This is brilliant fun!"

Kirsty nodded. "I know," she replied. Then she looked up and saw that there was a new glitter ball hanging from the ceiling – an extra-sparkly, *green* glitter

ball that sent thousands of jade green lights whirling around the hall as it spun.

"I love helping the fairies," Kirsty said to Rachel, pointing out the glitter ball with a grin. "And I can't wait to find another one of the Dance Ribbons!"

Rebecca the Rock 'n' Roll Fairy

by Daisy Meadows

Contents

Rock 'n' Roll Party

"Are you ready yet, Mum?" Kirsty Tate called up the stairs. "Rachel and I are dying to see your costumes!" She grinned over at her best friend, Rachel Walker, who was standing next to her.

"We'll be down soon," Mrs Tate called back from the bedroom.

Kirsty and Rachel sat down on

the bottom stair to wait.

"I *wish* we were going to the rock 'n' roll party with Mum and Dad," Kirsty sighed. "It sounds like fun, *and* we might find Rebecca the Rock 'n' Roll Fairy's magic ribbon there!"

Rachel nodded. "The Dance Fairies are depending on us!" she reminded Kirsty.

Rachel and Kirsty had become friends with the fairies when they were holidaying on Rainspell Island, and now the girls were always eager to help whenever the fairies had a problem.

The main cause of trouble in Fairyland

was mean Jack Frost, helped by his naughty goblin servants. A few days earlier, Jack Frost had asked the Dance Fairies to visit his ice castle and teach his goblins how to dance. But it was all a trick, so that the goblins could steal the Dance Fairies' magic ribbons!

When the King and Queen of Fairyland had demanded that the ribbons be given back, Jack Frost had refused. Instead he'd sent seven of his goblins tumbling into the human world, each clutching one of the ribbons.

Now, during their half-term holiday, Kirsty and Rachel were helping the Dance Fairies to find their ribbons.

"We've made a good start," Kirsty remarked. "We've already found Bethany the Ballet Fairy's ribbon, and Jade the Disco Fairy's too."

"But if we don't find the rest, all the other kinds of dancing will keep on going wrong, and dancing won't be fun any more!" Rachel sighed.

"Yes, and I suppose the dancing at the rock 'n' roll party tonight will be spoiled since Rebecca's Rock 'n' Roll Ribbon is still missing," Kirsty replied with a worried frown.

"Bethany told us that the magic ribbons are attracted to their own kind of dancing, remember?" Rachel pointed out. "So maybe the goblin who has Rebecca's ribbon will be at the rock 'n' roll party himself!"

"Girls, we're ready!" Mr Tate yelled from upstairs and Kirsty and Rachel turned round.

Mr and Mrs Tate came downstairs, and the girls' eyes widened with delight. Kirsty's dad was wearing jeans and a black leather jacket, and his hair was gelled into a quiff at the front. Kirsty's mum was wearing a white circular skirt, embroidered with black musical notes and a black top. She had a high ponytail, which was tied up with a red ribbon.

"You both look *fantastic*!" Kirsty gasped.

"You look like you just walked out of the film *Grease*!" Rachel added. "Will everyone be dressed up like you?"

Mr Tate nodded. "There's also going to be demonstrations of rock 'n' roll dancing," he explained, "and an Elvis Presley impersonator. Elvis was a famous rock 'n' roll singer, you see."

"And Kirsty's Uncle John is in charge of the music," Mrs Tate told Rachel. "We're taking some of our own rock 'n' roll records for him to play."

"It sounds like fun," Kirsty said wistfully.

"Well, why don't you two come

along?" Mrs Tate suggested with a smile. "We didn't ask you before because there aren't going to be any other young people there, but you might enjoy it."

Kirsty and Rachel looked thrilled.

"Can we?" Kirsty asked eagerly. "But what about Gran? She was going to come and look after us."

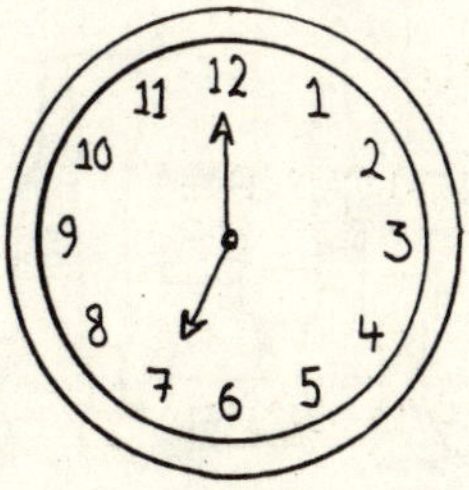

"She won't have left home yet," Mrs Tate said, glancing at the clock. "I'll give her a ring."

"Does it matter that we don't have costumes?" asked Rachel.

"Not at all," Mr Tate assured her.

"Isn't this great?" Kirsty whispered to Rachel as they went to grab their coats.

"We're going to the rock 'n' roll party after all!"

"Yes, and maybe we'll find Rebecca's Rock 'n' Roll Ribbon!" Rachel replied excitedly.

Rebecca in a Spin

After Mrs Tate had rung Kirsty's gran, they all set off for the village hall where the rock 'n' roll party was being held. As they walked inside and took off their coats, the girls looked eagerly around. Everyone was dressed up in rock 'n' roll outfits, and rock 'n' roll music was playing in the background. The hall was filled with round tables and chairs, apart from a large space in the middle which had been kept free for dancing, and there was also a refreshments table selling food and drink. At the opposite end of the hall was a brightly-lit stage.

"Who's *that*?" Rachel asked curiously, pointing to a man on the stage who was busy setting up a microphone. The man had dark hair and bushy sideburns, and he was

wearing a sparkly white jumpsuit.

"Oh, that's the Elvis impersonator," Mrs Tate explained. "He'll be singing later on."

"We'll pick up some drinks and snacks for us all and then find a table," said Mr Tate. "Would you girls mind taking these records over to John? He's over there by the record decks."

Mr Tate handed the box of records to Kirsty and then

he and Mrs Tate went to join the queue at the refreshments table.

Meanwhile, Rachel and Kirsty made their way across the hall. The record decks, connected to some very large speakers, were set up next to the stage, and boxes of records had been laid out in neat rows, but there was no sign of Kirsty's uncle.

"I wonder where Uncle John is?" Kirsty remarked.

"I'm right here!" A fair-haired man who looked very similar to Mr Tate popped up from under the table. "I was just fixing a loose wire. How are you, Kirsty?"

"I'm fine, Uncle John." Kirsty grinned, handing over the box of records. "This is my friend Rachel."

"Ah, the famous Rachel!" Uncle John exclaimed. "I've heard a lot about you! Excuse me for a moment, girls," he

went on quickly, "I must get the next record ready to start."

Kirsty and Rachel watched as Uncle John put another record on one of the decks.

"Ladies and gentlemen!" came an announcement at that moment. "May I have your attention please?"

There was a burst of applause and Kirsty and Rachel swung round to look up at the Elvis impersonator on the stage. "I'd like to welcome you all to our rock 'n' roll party!" Elvis went on. "We've got a fantastic night's entertainment lined up. And first on stage

are Linda and Will Melling, who are going to show us how to dance rock 'n' roll style."

As Linda and Will walked onto the stage in their sparkly rock 'n' roll outfits, the girls exchanged a worried glance.

"I hope their dance goes OK without the magic ribbon," Kirsty whispered.

"Yes, I'm crossing my fingers!" Rachel whispered back.

Uncle John lowered the needle onto the record and the music began. The song had a very fast beat, and Linda and Will started off by holding hands and doing a complicated series of steps involving lots of twists and turns around the stage.

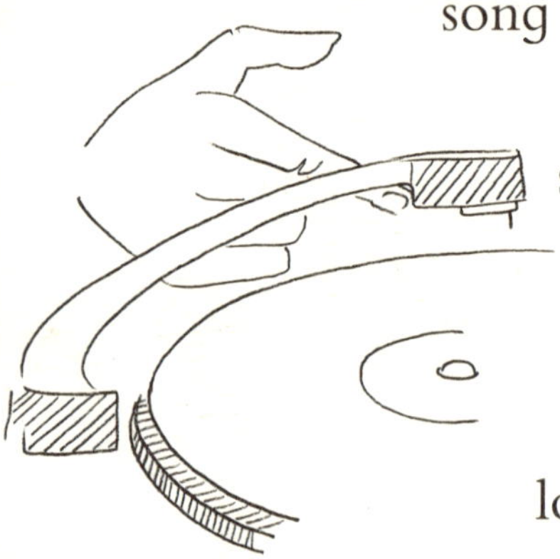

"I don't know anything about rock 'n' roll dancing, but this looks great to me!" Rachel murmured to Kirsty.

But right at that moment Linda suddenly stumbled. She managed to regain her balance quickly and smiled brightly at the audience, but the next second Will tripped, stubbing the toes of his left foot on the floor.

"Ow!" he yelled, and then quickly looked very embarrassed.

Linda tried to cover up the mistake by twirling across the stage in front of him, but unfortunately she stepped clumsily on Will's other foot as she did so.

"Ouch!" Will gasped.

"Oh, no!" Kirsty groaned as Will and Linda danced on, looking rather red. "This is all because Rebecca's ribbon is missing!"

Rachel nodded. The girls watched

anxiously, hoping nothing else would happen, but it soon became clear that neither Linda nor Will could remember their steps. Linda went left when she should have gone right, Will went right when he should have gone left, and they ended up bumping heavily into each other. Then, as Linda jumped into Will's arms and he tried to lift her above his head, they collapsed in an

ungainly heap on the stage.

The audience looked shocked and the Elvis impersonator rushed out of the wings to help the dazed dancers to their feet. After a murmured conversation between the three of them, Elvis grabbed the microphone again.

"Linda and Will are going to take a quick break," he announced, looking rather flustered. "They'll be back for

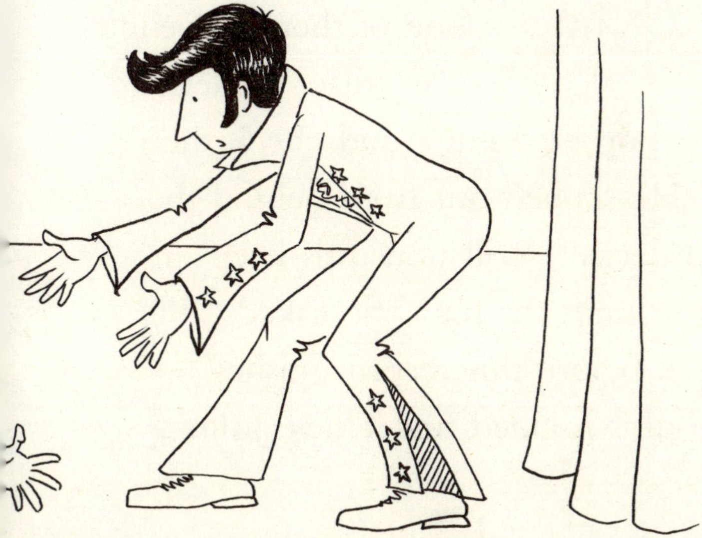

another performance later on."

Looking very embarrassed, Linda and Will fled from the stage as everyone applauded politely. Kirsty and Rachel felt very sorry for them.

"I don't understand it!" Uncle John said in confusion, as he put another record on. "Linda and Will are usually brilliant! Maybe one of them is feeling ill or something. I'll just pop backstage and check they're OK." He slipped out from behind the record decks. "Will you girls keep an eye on things for me?" he asked. "I'll be back before this record finishes."

The girls nodded and Uncle John

hurried off.

"Poor Linda and Will," Kirsty sighed. "This is all because of mean old Jack Frost and his goblins!"

"Hello!" called a tiny, silvery voice suddenly.

Rachel grabbed Kirsty's arm. "Did you hear that?" she gasped.

Kirsty nodded. "But where's it coming from?" she asked, glancing around.

"I'm down here!" the voice called.

Rachel and Kirsty looked down at the record decks. There, sitting on the edge of the record that was spinning around on the turntable, was a tiny, sparkling fairy.

"Oh!" Kirsty exclaimed. "It's Rebecca the Rock 'n' Roll Fairy!"

A Glimpse of Goblins

"Hi, girls!" called Rebecca, beaming all over her pretty face. She wore a purple scoop-necked top, a circular black skirt embroidered with big pink spots, and a matching pink scarf around her neck. Her long brown hair was tied up in a ponytail, just like Mrs Tate's.

"Hi, Rebecca!" Rachel and Kirsty

whispered as the little fairy fluttered daintily off the spinning record.

"What are you doing here?" added Kirsty eagerly. "Is your ribbon nearby?"

Rebecca nodded. "I think so," she said in a low voice. "I can *feel* it, but it can't be very close, otherwise poor Linda and Will wouldn't have danced so badly."

Rachel and Kirsty nodded. They knew that when a magic ribbon was very close by, everyone danced beautifully.

"Girls, we must find the ribbon before Linda and Will go back on stage," Rebecca said in a determined voice.

"Then my lovely rock 'n' roll dancing will be perfect! Will you help me look for the goblin? He must be around here *some*where."

"Of course we will," Kirsty replied. But just then she saw Uncle John heading back towards them. "Rebecca, here comes my uncle! You'd better hide."

Rebecca immediately flew to hide on Rachel's shoulder behind her hair.

"Looks like Will and Linda are absolutely fine now," Uncle John said cheerfully.

"I've just watched them practising backstage, and they were brilliant! I think they must have had a bad attack of nerves earlier."

"This is very strange!" Rebecca whispered to Rachel. "My ribbon's missing, but Will and Linda are dancing properly again. That can only mean one thing..."

"...the ribbon's backstage!" Rachel finished for her in a low voice.

Kirsty heard her and looked excited. "Let's go backstage right away, then, and find the goblin!" she whispered.

There was a door at the side of the stage and the girls made their way over to it, leaving Uncle John to put on another record.

They were worried that someone might notice them, but luckily people were too busy chatting and buying refreshments. Quite a few couples were already on the dance floor, including Mr and Mrs Tate. But just like Will and Linda, they all kept bumping into each other, treading on toes and forgetting their steps.

"This party will be a disaster if I don't find my ribbon!" Rebecca sighed as Kirsty opened the door.

Rebecca, Rachel and Kirsty found Will and Linda practising their moves in a room behind the stage. The two dancers seemed like a different couple from the clumsy, awkward duo who had performed earlier. Now their kicks and twirls were completely in time and they didn't make a single mistake.

"Uncle John was right!" Kirsty said admiringly, as Will flipped Linda high up into the air and then caught her again. "They are amazing!"

"My ribbon is in here somewhere!" Rebecca said eagerly. "I can sense it!"

Rachel glanced around and suddenly noticed that one of the cupboard doors behind them stood slightly ajar. As she stared at it, she saw a knobbly green foot poke out through the gap, just for a second, before it quickly disappeared again.

"Kirsty! Rebecca!" Rachel whispered excitedly. "There's a goblin inside that cupboard!"

Goblins Revealed!

"Are you sure?" Rebecca asked.

Rachel nodded. "I saw his foot poking out," she explained.

"We can't do anything about the goblin while Will and Linda are here," Kirsty said. "We'll have to wait until they've finished practising."

The girls watched as Will and Linda

worked on their finale. Will threw Linda up into the air again, where she turned a double somersault and landed in Will's arms before lowering herself into the splits.

"That's much better!" Will beamed at his partner. "I don't know *what* went wrong before."

"Yes, it was *so* embarrassing!" Linda groaned.

"Let's get a drink before we go back on stage," Will suggested, and they hurried off, giving the girls a friendly smile as they went.

Immediately Rebecca flew out from behind Rachel's hair and the three friends dashed over to the cupboard.

"Be careful, Kirsty!" Rachel warned as her friend reached for the door handle. "Remember that Jack Frost has given the goblins freezing powers!"

Carefully Kirsty pulled the door open and the girls peered inside.

The cupboard was crammed with music stands, old props from plays, and *two* goblins squashed one behind the other. The goblin at the front was clutching a sparkly purple ribbon in his hand.

When they saw the girls the goblins both let out a loud shriek of annoyance.

"Go away!" yelled the one with the ribbon, trying to pull the door closed again. "You can't see us! We're hiding!"

The other one scowled, grabbed the head from a pantomime horse and put it over his own head. "Now you can't see me!" he said in a muffled voice. "Go away!"

But Kirsty shook her head firmly.

"I'm not going anywhere until I get my magic ribbon back!" Rebecca said, hovering in the doorway.

The first goblin looked nervous.

"Don't come near me!" he shrieked. "I don't want to be frozen!"

Rachel, Kirsty and Rebecca glanced at each other in confusion.

"You idiot!" the second goblin said, pulling the horse's head off and poking his friend hard in the ribs. "*We're* the ones who can freeze people as long as we have a magic ribbon, *not* them!"

"Oh, yes!" said the first goblin, "I forgot." Then his face darkened. "And don't poke me or I'll poke you harder!"

Rachel was staring at the second

goblin. "That's the goblin who stole Bethany's Ballet Ribbon!" she whispered to Kirsty.

"I think he's recognised us too!" Kirsty whispered back as the second goblin glared at them.

"Never mind about me!" the second goblin yelled as the first goblin gave him a sharp poke in the ribs. "You should be freezing the pesky fairy and her human friends."

"Ooh, yes!" said the first goblin eagerly.

"I'll turn you into fairies, girls," Rebecca called, quickly lifting her wand as the first goblin lunged out of the cupboard towards them.

"Go on, freeze them all!" the second goblin sniggered, tumbling out after his friend.

A shower of magic dust from Rebecca's wand fell softly around Rachel and Kirsty and transformed them into fairies in the twinkling of an eye. Immediately the girls fluttered their gauzy wings and flew up into the air out of the goblin's reach.

"Oh, I *hate* it when they do that!"

the first goblin said crossly. He started jumping up into the air, trying to touch Rachel, Kirsty and Rebecca and shouting "Freeze!" but he missed every time.

"What shall we do now?" Rachel asked as they hovered above the goblins' heads. "We still have to get the ribbon back somehow."

"It's going to be hard with two goblins," said Rebecca anxiously.

Kirsty frowned at the two goblins below. The first one was still leaping up and down and shouting "Freeze!" at them, although they were well out of his reach.

"Maybe we could get the first goblin to freeze the second one?" she suggested. "We just have to make sure they're touching each other when the first goblin says 'Freeze!'."

"That's a great idea!" Rebecca said with a big grin. "Let's lead them into it. On the count of three – one, two, three!"

Linking hands, Rachel, Kirsty and Rebecca immediately flew down and hovered near the second goblin. With a shriek of triumph the first goblin rushed towards them. The girls waited until the last possible moment and then zoomed upwards out of reach.

"Freeze!" shouted the first goblin, just as he collided heavily with his friend.

The Magic Singing Stick

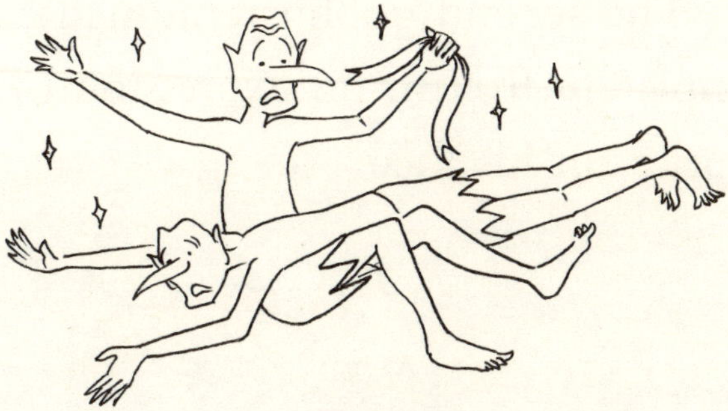

Instantly the second goblin was frozen solid. The first goblin landed on the ground and his frozen friend fell over too, and landed in his lap. The first goblin looked so shocked, the girls and Rebecca couldn't help laughing.

"Oh, no!" the first goblin groaned, pushing his frozen friend off him so that he could stand up. Then he stood the second goblin up too and examined him carefully. He poked and prodded him hard. He even tried breathing warm air onto him, but it was no use. The second goblin remained completely frozen, an expression of surprise on his face.

"So now we only have one goblin to deal with!" said Rebecca. "How shall we make him give my ribbon back?"

Before the girls could answer, they heard the sound of music coming from the stage behind them. The Elvis impersonator had started singing and the slow, beautiful melody caught their attention.

"Oh!" Kirsty said suddenly, "I know this! It's a famous song by Elvis Presley called *Love Me* Tender. My dad plays it all the time."

"I think the goblin likes it too!" Rachel whispered.

The first goblin had stopped trying to thaw out his friend. Instead he was swaying to the music, his head cocked on one side, an expression of enchantment on his face.

"I've never heard such beautiful music!" he said dreamily, waving the magic ribbon and beginning to dance.

"He can't help but dance to rock 'n' roll music while he's holding my ribbon," Rebecca laughed as the goblin danced his way closer to the back of the stage. "We'd better go after him, girls!"

"What about the frozen goblin?" asked Rachel, "We can't leave him here. Somebody might come along and see him!"

Rebecca waved her wand and the frozen goblin floated gently into the air and into the props cupboard, the door closing behind him. The other goblin was now standing in the wings, still swaying dreamily and staring in awe at the Elvis impersonator.

"Love me tender," the goblin croaked loudly, trying to sing along.

"He's terrible!" Rachel whispered.

"We must stop him before someone hears!" Kirsty added urgently.

"Just be careful because he can still freeze us," Rebecca warned as they zoomed towards the goblin. "Although I think the music has made him forget all about his freezing powers."

The girls and Rebecca hovered around the goblin's head, but he didn't even notice them until Rebecca tapped him on the shoulder with her wand.

"It's better if you just listen," said Rachel. "Elvis will stop singing if he thinks everyone wants to sing instead of listening to him."

The goblin shut up immediately. "I don't want him to stop," he sighed happily.

"Do you like singing?" asked Kirsty.

The goblin nodded. "But goblins

aren't any good at singing," he said in a sad voice. "I think it's because we don't have magic singing sticks like the man on the stage."

"Magic singing sticks?" Kirsty repeated, confused.

"Yes, *a*ll the best singers have them!" the goblin said impatiently. "I've seen them on TV in the human world."

"He means a microphone," Rachel whispered. And as she said that, an idea popped right into her head. Quickly she drew Rebecca and Kirsty aside.

"We can see how much the goblin wants to sing like Elvis," she pointed out. "Rebecca, do you think you could magic up a microphone that makes everyone who sings into it sound like Elvis? I'm sure the goblin would swap the magic ribbon for *that*!"

"Of course I can!" Rebecca nodded. "The microphone won't last for ever, though. It will dissolve into fairy dust after a few hours."

"That should be long enough," said Rachel. "I'm sure the goblin will have lots of fun with the microphone while it lasts." And she swooped down to whisper in the goblin's ear. "Would *you* like to sound like Elvis?" Rachel asked.

The goblin nodded eagerly.

"Well, we can give you a magic singing stick of your very own!" Kirsty joined in. "Follow us!"

Rebecca and the girls led the goblin right away from the stage and into an empty room. First Rebecca scattered purple fairy dust over Rachel and Kirsty to make them human again. Then, with another flick of her wand, a tall, shining silver microphone appeared in a burst of purple sparkles.

"Oh!" The goblin clapped his hands in delight. "How does it work?"

Rachel went over to the microphone. "You sing into this bit and it makes you sound like Elvis," she explained.

Rachel sang *Love Me Tender* into the microphone and was rather surprised when her voice came out deep and manly and just like Elvis Presley's, right down to the American accent!

Kirsty and Rebecca laughed.

"Ooh! I want it!" the goblin shrieked excitedly, jumping up and down. "Give me the magic singing stick RIGHT NOW!"

Rockin' Goblin

"We'll swap the magic singing stick for the magic ribbon," Kirsty said. "But you know this kind of fairy magic doesn't last for ever. In a few hours it'll dissolve away into fairy dust."

The goblin barely hesitated. "That's OK," he said, shoving the ribbon at Rachel and grabbing the microphone stand.

Rebecca gave a little squeal of delight. She immediately shrank the ribbon down to its Fairyland size and it floated out of Rachel's hand to reattach itself to her wand.

As it did so, the ribbon glowed a deeper shade of purple and was briefly surrounded by a faint mist of lavender sparkles.

Just then the second goblin rushed into the room.

"He's thawed out!" Rachel whispered. "We got the ribbon back just in time!"

The second goblin glared at his friend.

"Why has that pesky fairy got her ribbon back?" he demanded.

"I swapped it for this magic singing stick!" the first goblin explained, stroking the silver microphone proudly.

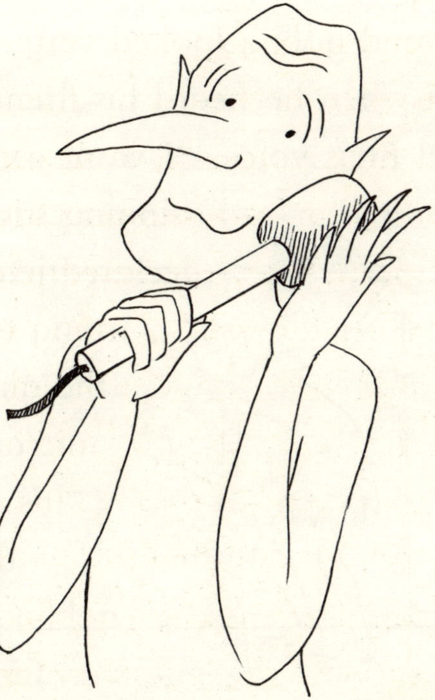

"What?" shrieked the second goblin furiously. "What's Jack Frost going to say when he finds out you've swapped the magic ribbon for a silly silver stick?"

"It's not silly!" the first goblin snapped indignantly. "Listen!" And he began to sing.

The second goblin looked very impressed when he heard his friend's wonderful Elvis voice. "I want a magic singing stick!" he declared jealously, trying to grab the glittering microphone.

"It's mine!" the first goblin roared furiously.

And, picking up the microphone, he dashed off with the other goblin in hot pursuit.

"I think that's the last we've seen of them for tonight!" Rebecca laughed. "Girls, I simply can't thank you enough. You've been amazing!" She grinned happily at Kirsty and Rachel. "And now I must go straight back to Fairyland and tell everyone the good news!"

Just then they heard the sound of applause from the hall.

"Linda and Will are back on stage," Rebecca went on. "And their rock 'n' roll dance should go well now that I've got my ribbon back." She waved her wand at the girls and the magic ribbon sparkled. "Good luck with finding the other ribbons, and keep a sharp look-out for more goblins, girls!" Rebecca called, and then she vanished in a puff of purple sparkles as the girls waved goodbye.

Kirsty and Rachel rushed back into the hall to join Mr and Mrs Tate. They were just in time to see

Will and Linda launch into a very complicated routine of steps, kicks and twists which they performed with perfect timing, neither of them missing a beat. Then Will lifted Linda high over his head and there was a gasp of amazement from the audience as she jumped right over him and landed neatly on the other side.

Rachel and Kirsty grinned at each other.

"Everything's fine now that Rebecca's got her rock 'n' roll ribbon back," Rachel whispered.

"But there are still *four* ribbons to find," Kirsty pointed out with a smile. "I wonder what our next fairy adventure will be?"

Tasha the Ballet Fairy

by Daisy Meadows

Contents

Tapping Trouble

"Wow," Kirsty Tate said, as she followed her mum through the door of Wetherbury College's main hall and saw the crowds inside. "It's really busy in here!"

Her friend, Rachel Walker, who was staying with Kirsty over half-term, nodded in agreement, as she took off her woolly hat and stuffed it in her pocket. "There's a pottery stand," she said, pointing it out. "Ooh, and look, they're decorating cakes over there!"

The girls had come with Kirsty's mum to the college Open Day. This was a special event where people could come and find out more about all the different

courses the college offered. Since Mrs Tate attended a wood-carving class at the college, she'd volunteered to help out on the wood-carving stand and answer any questions people might have. All around the hall there were other display stands showing different skills you could learn at the college.

"There's the wood-carving stand," Mrs Tate said, showing the girls. "That's where I'll be all morning, OK? But you can wander round and look at everything else. There's lots to see."

Rachel and Kirsty said goodbye and set off around the hall. They saw a man at the pottery stand making a vase on a potter's wheel, and then watched as a make-up artist transformed somebody into a ghoul at the special-effects make-up stand. It was amazing how the thick white make-up and some fake blood running down his chin made the volunteer look completely different.

"Spooky," Kirsty whispered to Rachel with a shudder.

The make-up artist smiled at the girls. "You can create almost anything with the right make-up," she told them.

The 'ghoul' grinned. "It's pretty strange being turned into something else, though!" he said.

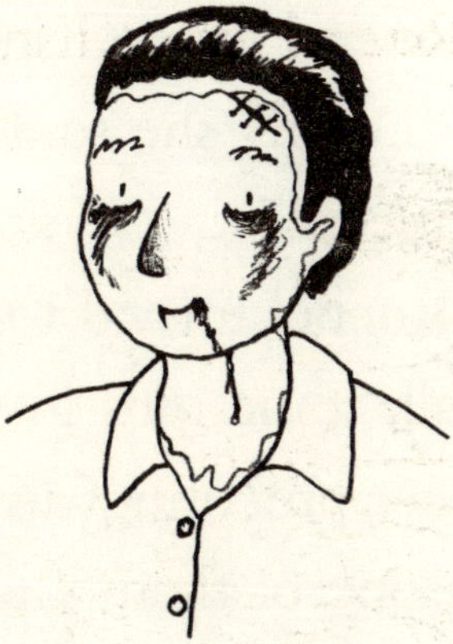

Rachel and Kirsty exchanged a smile. They knew all about being turned into *something* else. Thanks to their fairy friends, they'd been turned into fairies many times!

Only a few days earlier, Rachel and Kirsty had been plunged into another fairy adventure, this time helping the

Dance Fairies find their missing magic Dance Ribbons. So far, the girls had helped find three of the ribbons, but four others were still lost.

Just as Rachel was thinking about the Dance Fairies, Kirsty nudged her.

"Look!" she said pointing. "Tap dancers!"

Rachel turned to see. At the end of the hall, some girls in sparkly red tap shoes were practising a routine. Rachel winced as one of them clumsily dropped her black cane on another dancer's foot, and the girl next to her promptly tripped over it.

"Kirsty, did you see that?" she hissed. "The dancing is going wrong already!"

Kirsty nodded. "And we both know why," she replied. "It's because Tasha the Tap Dance Fairy's ribbon is still missing!"

The girls had learned that the Dance Fairies used their ribbons to make sure that dancing, both in Fairyland and in the human world, went as smoothly as possible. Unfortunately, Jack Frost, a bad fairy, had stolen the magic ribbons because he wanted his goblin servants to dance well at his parties.

When the Fairy King and Queen heard that the Dance Ribbons had been stolen, they went straight to Jack Frost's ice castle to get them back, but selfish Jack Frost saw them approaching and flung the ribbons into the human world, along with a goblin to guard each one.

Without their ribbons, the Dance Fairies could not work their special magic, and dancing everywhere was going horribly wrong.

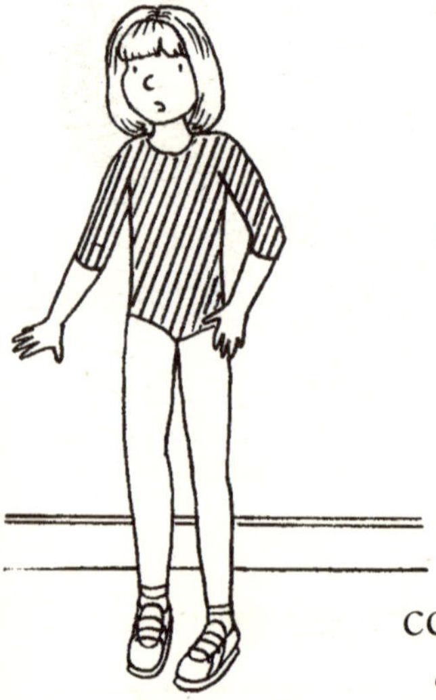

"Excuse me," came a voice from behind the girls.

Rachel and Kirsty turned to see a girl of about their age, dressed in a leotard like the other tap dancers.

"Have you seen a pair of red tap shoes and a black cane anywhere?" she asked. "I won't be able to join in the performance if I don't find them."

Kirsty shook her head. "Sorry, we haven't seen them," she replied.

The girl sighed. "Maybe they fell out of my bag in the car park when Mum dropped me off," she said.

"We'll go and look for them if you want," Rachel offered.

The girl's eyes brightened. "Oh, thank you," she said. "I'll carry on looking in here. I'm Ashleigh Hart, by the way."

"We're Kirsty and Rachel," Kirsty replied, smiling, as Ashleigh waved and set off to search the rest of the hall.

Kirsty and Rachel turned towards the entrance, but then stopped as they both heard a faint tapping sound which was in perfect time to the tap dancers' music. Rachel looked over at the dancers eagerly. Did this mean the magic ribbon was nearby, helping the dancers to improve?

But the dancers weren't actually dancing at all! *If they're not making the*

tapping sound, then who is? Rachel wondered.

Tap-tap-tap-tappity-TAP! Tap-tap-tap-tappity-TAP!

"I think it's coming from over here," Kirsty said, walking towards the corner of the hall.

Rachel followed. There was nothing there except a table with some leaflets on it, but the tapping definitely got louder as she and Kirsty approached. Curiously, the girls peeped underneath the table.

Tasha Turns Up

Rachel and Kirsty smiled to see a tiny fairy, with her eyes closed, tap dancing her way through an amazing routine at super-speed! It was Tasha the Tap Dance Fairy, of course! Nobody else would have been able to dance so brilliantly with the Tap Dance Ribbon missing. The fairy wore a smart-looking black waistcoat, black tights, tap shoes, and a bright red skirt.

Kirsty gave a polite cough and Tasha's eyes snapped open. "Oh, hello," she said. "You caught me out. I just couldn't resist dancing when I heard the music."

"You're really good!" Rachel told her. "I've never seen anyone tap dance so fast before."

Tasha smiled. "Thanks," she said. "But it's a shame the other tap dancers are having problems."

She sighed. "If only my Tap Dance Ribbon were safely back on my wand where it belongs, then they wouldn't keep tripping up!"

"Have you any idea where your ribbon is?" Kirsty asked.

Tasha shook her head. "No," she said. "I haven't sensed it yet but I'm hoping it might be around here. Keep your eyes open for any goblins, girls!"

Rachel glanced nervously around. The goblins were Jack Frost's sneaky servants, and she and Kirsty had managed to outwit them in the past.

This time, though, Jack Frost had given the goblins a special power. As long as a goblin had one of the magic Dance Ribbons, he also had the power to freeze people.

Kirsty and Rachel never liked meeting the goblins, but now they felt warier than ever about tackling them. Neither girl wanted to be turned into an ice cube!

"We were just about to go outside," Kirsty told Tasha. "One of the dancers has lost her shoes and cane and we said we'd help look for them."

Tasha looked thoughtful. "Lost her shoes and cane?" she repeated.

"I wonder if they're really lost, or if somebody has pinched them!"

"Like a goblin?" Rachel suggested at once. "It's just the sort of thing a goblin would do!"

Tasha nodded, her eyes sparkling. "We'd better keep an eye out for goblins while we're looking for the shoes and cane," she said.

"Maybe we'll find the Tap Dance Ribbon too," Kirsty added hopefully. She pulled her coat pocket open. "Tasha, do you want to hop in here?"

Tasha fluttered out from under the table, her gauzy wings shimmering under the bright lights of the hall, and dived into Kirsty's pocket. "Let's go!" she said eagerly.

As the girls walked outside, Kirsty wound her scarf a little tighter around her neck, and Rachel pulled her woolly hat back on to keep her ears warm.

The college car park was directly in front of them. "Let's walk around the

edges," Kirsty suggested. "A pair of red tap shoes shouldn't be too hard to spot."

Kirsty and Rachel set off around the car park, keeping a careful eye out for the shoes and cane, as well as any cars that might be driving about. They were also half expecting to see a flash of green and a scuttling goblin, but there was no sign of any goblin mischief.

Suddenly, Tasha zoomed out of Kirsty's pocket and spun in the air excitedly, gazing out around the car park. "I can sense my ribbon!" she declared. "I'm sure it's somewhere nearby."

By now, the girls had done a full

circuit of the car park and were back outside the main entrance. Rachel pointed to a path leading around the side of the college. "How about looking down there?" she suggested.

Tasha nodded. "Good idea," she agreed. "My ribbon can't be far away."

The three friends walked along the footpath.

They could hear the tap dance music again now, drifting out of an open window.

"What was that?" Tasha whispered suddenly, hovering in the air in front of the girls.

Rachel and Kirsty stopped to listen. Kirsty couldn't hear anything except the music at first, but then she heard a *tap-tap-tap-tappity-tap* in perfect time to the rhythm.

"Those are definitely tap shoes!" Rachel said excitedly.

"And the tapping isn't coming from inside the hall," Tasha added. "So it must be somebody else!"

"The goblin!" Kirsty and Rachel whispered at the same time.

The girls crept a little further down the path and peered cautiously around the next corner.

There before them, tapping away and humming to the music, was a goblin. On his feet were sparkly red tap shoes, and in his hand was a cane with Tasha's magic ribbon attached to it.

The Big Freeze

"What does he *look* like?" Tasha muttered, stifling a laugh. "Come on," she said to Kirsty and Rachel. "Let's go and get my ribbon back!"

Kirsty, Rachel and Tasha headed over to the goblin who was far too busy dancing to notice them.

"I'll have my ribbon back now,

please," Tasha said in a firm voice.

The goblin jumped in surprise, then glared at her. "Can't you see I'm trying to dance?" he asked crossly. "I've lost my place now!" He rolled his eyes irritably, then turned away and began tapping again.

"Well, tough, because we've come to get the cane and shoes back, too," Kirsty told him. "They don't belong to you!"

The goblin stamped his foot and spun around. "You're ruining my concentration!" he screamed. "How am I meant to dance when I keep on getting interrupted? If you must watch, please do so quietly!"

"I've had enough of this!" Tasha snapped. "It's not your ribbon to be dancing with. Give it back!"

Just then, someone must have turned the volume up in the hall, because the music suddenly got louder. The goblin launched into another routine, twirling his cane deftly in his hand as he tapped his feet.

He's good, Rachel thought, but she knew he was only dancing well because he had the magic ribbon close to him.

The Dance Ribbons were so powerful, that they could turn even the clumsiest dancer into something special if they were close enough.

The goblin seemed totally absorbed in his dancing. His eyes were screwed shut in concentration as he tapped away. Gradually, he started drifting away from the three friends and towards the music and a side door into the college.

"What's he doing?" Kirsty hissed anxiously. "Someone will see him, if he's not careful."

"I thought the goblins were supposed to be hiding," Rachel said in a low voice. "But he's not even trying."

Tasha grinned. "That's because of the ribbon," she explained. "It draws whoever has it towards music, making them dance whenever they hear a tune. Once they're dancing, they forget about everything else!"

"Well, hopefully he'll forget about *us*," Kirsty said, hurrying after the goblin. "And then we can grab the ribbon while he's distracted."

The girls and Tasha followed the goblin right up to the door, but as he opened it and danced through the entrance, he noticed them and stopped.

"Are you still here?" he snapped. "Well, I'm warning you, don't come any closer or I'll freeze you!"

And with that, he slipped through the door and slammed it shut, right in the girls' faces!

"Hey!" cried Kirsty indignantly. She ran to the door and turned the handle but the door seemed to be shut tight.

"Oh, no!" she cried. "It won't open! We'll lose him!"

"It's OK, there's a window open up there," Tasha said, pointing. "I'll fly in and keep track of him."

Rachel pushed against the door with Kirsty as Tasha zipped in through the open window. "Has he locked it, do you think?" she panted.

"I don't know. Whoooa!" cried Kirsty as the door suddenly gave way.

She and Rachel tumbled inside just in time to see Tasha waving her wand. A stream of fairy magic whizzed through the air and over to the Tap Dance Ribbon, which immediately began to unravel itself from the cane in the goblin's hand. Rachel and Kirsty watched excitedly as Tasha made a dive to grab it.

But, at that same moment, the goblin leapt up and touched the fairy with one gnarly green finger. "FREEZE!" he shouted, and, to the girls' horror, Tasha instantly turned to ice.

No longer able to fly, the little fairy plummeted towards the ground like a stone.

Tasha's Tumble

As Tasha tumbled towards the floor, Rachel whipped off her woolly hat and dived forwards, holding the hat out in front of her. Fortunately, Rachel was just in time to catch Tasha softly in the hat before the frozen fairy hit the floor.

The goblin didn't seem to care. He just gave a mean cackle. "You pesky girls will be next unless you leave me alone," he told them. "So stay away!"

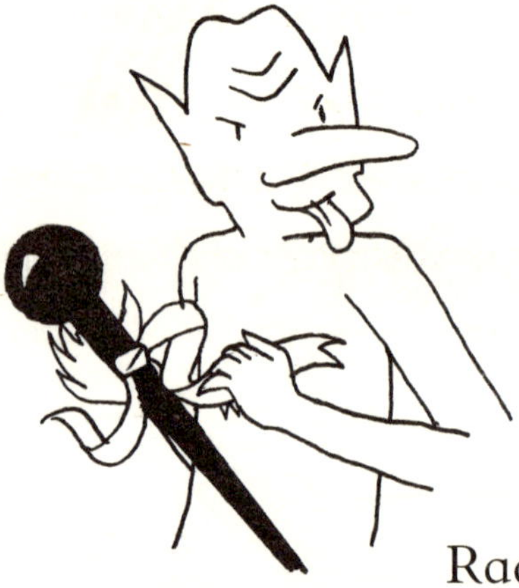

Then he stuck his tongue out, tightened the ribbon around his cane and danced off down the corridor.

Rachel looked down at Tasha who was still frozen rigid in the hat. The fairy's dark hair twinkled with frost, and her face had an icy blue tinge to it.

"Oh, Tasha," Rachel said, blowing on her gently to try

and warm her up. "Tasha, can you hear me?"

"How about holding her in your hands?" Kirsty suggested. "They might be warmer than the hat."

Rachel agreed and carefully scooped the frozen fairy into her cupped palm. But, at that very moment, the girls heard footsteps coming along the corridor, and before Rachel could even think about hiding Tasha, a woman appeared.

Kirsty gulped. How on earth were they going to explain away a frozen fairy?

Before she could think of anything to say, the woman began to speak.

"What a lovely ice sculpture!" she cried, peering at Tasha. "So delicate! So lifelike! I hadn't realised the college offered an ice-sculpting course as well."

Rachel could only manage a small smile in response and both girls heaved a sigh of relief as the lady smiled back and went on her way.

"Phew," Rachel said. "That was close!"

Kirsty was about to reply when a tiny, fairy-sized sneeze came from Tasha. Both girls looked down hopefully and beamed as Tasha opened her eyes, shivered, and stood up on Rachel's hand, rubbing her arms.

"Tasha! Are you all right?" Kirsty asked anxiously.

Tasha sneezed three more times, flapped her wings tentatively and then smiled. "I'm fine," she said. "Luckily, the goblins' freezing power isn't strong enough to freeze anyone for long. The magic soon wears off. And now I'm more determined than ever to get my Tap Dance Ribbon back!"

Rachel nodded. "Come on," she said. "Let's find that goblin!"

Tasha flew back into Kirsty's pocket

and the girls set off down the corridor, in the same direction that the goblin had taken. On their way, they caught a brief glimpse of Ashleigh in one of the classrooms, still hunting for her missing things.

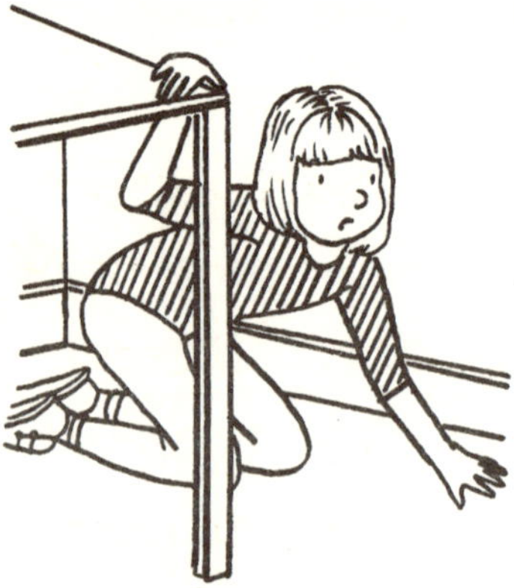

"I hope she doesn't see you-know-who wearing her shoes," Kirsty muttered to Rachel as they went past.

They reached the hall, where the music was still playing. Kirsty looked over to where the tap dancers had been practising and gasped in amazement as she realised who was dancing merrily along with them. It was the goblin!

"Look at him!" Kirsty squealed, shocked to see him in so public a place. "I can't believe nobody else has noticed him!"

Rachel stared hard. The goblin was *very* visible, tap dancing right in front of the speakers. "Oh, and look," she said, noticing something else. "The dancers around him are doing much better now. It must be because they're near the magic ribbon!"

The girls edged closer, not sure what to do. They wanted to grab the ribbon but they didn't want to draw any more attention to the goblin.

"Look at that little green chap!" they heard a man say just then.

"What a wonderful dancer!"

"He must have had his make-up done at the special-effects stand," the man's friend replied. "Is he supposed to be some kind of goblin, do you think?"

"Weird-looking, isn't he, with those great rubbery ears?" another person commented. "They can do marvellous things with make-up these days!"

Rachel had to clap her hand over her mouth to stop herself from giggling. And Kirsty, too, had to stifle a laugh.

"We've got to get him out of here," Tasha said. "It's all very well people thinking he's in costume, but what happens if someone realises that he really is a goblin?"

Kirsty nodded, looking serious again. "That would be a disaster," she agreed. "And what if Ashleigh comes back and sees him dancing with her shoes and cane?"

"I don't know," Rachel sighed, looking anxious. "He's desperate to be near the music. He's as close as he can possibly get to the speakers! How are we going to draw him away?"

Perfect Timing

Kirsty thought hard. The goblin was looking very pleased with himself. He was obviously enjoying his performance, and was even showing off to the other dancers! His cockiness gave her an idea.

"What if we persuade him to take part in a dance competition with you, Tasha?" she suggested. "I bet he won't be able to resist trying to prove that he's the better tap dancer!"

Tasha grinned. "That sounds like an excellent plan!" she agreed.

Kirsty and Rachel went over to the goblin, and Tasha popped her head out of Kirsty's pocket.

"Hey!" she called to the goblin. "You know, you're not *bad* at tap dancing, but you'll never be as good as me."

The goblin looked indignant. "*Not bad?*" he spluttered. "I'm the best tap dancer in the world!"

Tasha laughed. "No way," she replied. "I'm the Tap Dance Fairy. I'm obviously the best!"

The goblin stopped dancing and stamped his foot. "No, *I* am!" he snapped.

Kirsty interrupted. "Why don't you two have a competition to settle it?" she suggested.

"Yes, if you're as good as you think you are, you should be able to follow Tasha's steps," Rachel told the goblin. "Or are you worried she'll be better than you?"

"No chance!" the goblin snorted. "OK, I'll do it and I'll win!"

Kirsty smiled. "Oh, and there's one more thing," she added. "If you're better than Tasha, we'll stop bothering you about the Tap Dance Ribbon and you can keep it. But if you lose, you have to give it back."

The goblin hesitated, looking suspiciously from Tasha to Kirsty.

"Worried I'll win, are you?" Tasha teased.

The goblin snorted. "As if!" he retorted. "Of course you won't win. Let's do it!"

Rachel smiled. "Let's find an empty classroom," she suggested. "Then we'll have more space for dancing."

The girls, the goblin and Tasha all left the hall and found an empty room close by, where they could still hear the tap dance music.

Tasha hopped onto a desk. "Ready?" she asked the goblin. He nodded. "Then watch!"

She launched into a routine, tapping her tiny fairy heels and toes on the desktop, and finishing with a flourish of her cane.

"Easy," the goblin sneered, and he went on to copy her steps perfectly.

"OK," Tasha said. "Let's try another one." She tapped out a much more complicated routine.

This time the goblin simply shrugged. "No problem," he said, and copied the routine perfectly once more. "Is that the best you can do?" he smirked.

Tasha arched an eyebrow.

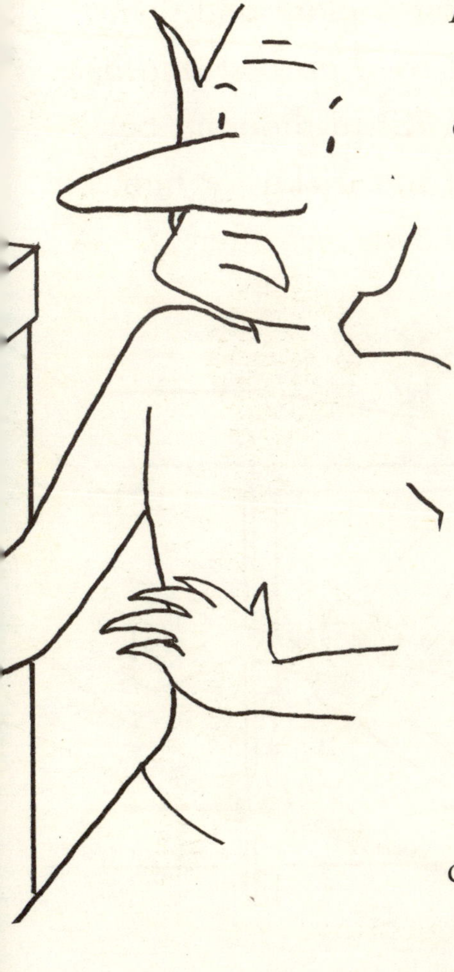

"I'll show you the best I can do," Tasha responded. And, with that, she threw herself into a third routine, her shoes tapping like fury on the desktop, her cane a blur as she twirled and twisted it in front of her. The goblin's mouth fell open as she finished. "Ta-dah!" Tasha cried, twirling her cane on one finger. The goblin gulped.

"Ready when you are," Rachel prompted.

The goblin shot her a glare and then began tapping. *He tried his best and he wasn't doing badly*, Kirsty thought, but the routine was just too tricky for him, and he fell over his own feet after a few moments.

Tasha smiled. "I win, I believe," she said, stretching out a hand for the ribbon.

The goblin shook his head, panting. "No," he argued. "That wasn't fair. The girls were putting me off, and...and these shoes were a bit tight, and..."

Rachel was outraged to hear so many excuses. "Tasha won the ribbon, fair and square!" she said.

Tasha gave Rachel and Kirsty a secret wink. "All right," she told the goblin. "I'll give you one last chance. I bet you can't do this!"

She began dancing again – and the girls could clearly see that it was a simpler routine this time. But, at the end, she tossed her cane high in the air with one hand, before catching it cleanly with the other. The fairy gave the girls a meaningful smile. *She's plotting something*, Kirsty thought, *but what?*

The goblin began to dance the routine, mimicking Tasha's steps exactly. The ribbon on the cane fluttered as he tapped his heart out.

And then, as the goblin neared the end of the routine, Rachel and Kirsty both realised what Tasha was planning.

She's hoping the goblin will toss the cane into the air, like she did, Kirsty thought. *And, if he does, maybe Rachel or I can catch it!*

Kirsty held her breath as the goblin tapped his last steps.

"Now!" Tasha shouted to the girls, as the goblin flipped the cane into the air.

Happy Tapping

Kirsty darted forward, her arm outstretched, her gaze fixed on the falling cane. The goblin realised he'd been caught out and he jumped up to try and catch the cane, too.

But Kirsty was taller and she got there first. "Got it!" she cheered, as her fingers closed around the cane.

Quickly, she detached the magic ribbon and gave it to Tasha, who shrank it down to its Fairyland size and reattached it to her wand. A flurry of sparkles and tiny top hats whirled around the wand as it met the ribbon, and the ribbon itself shimmered brightly with fairy magic.

"That's better!" Tasha beamed.

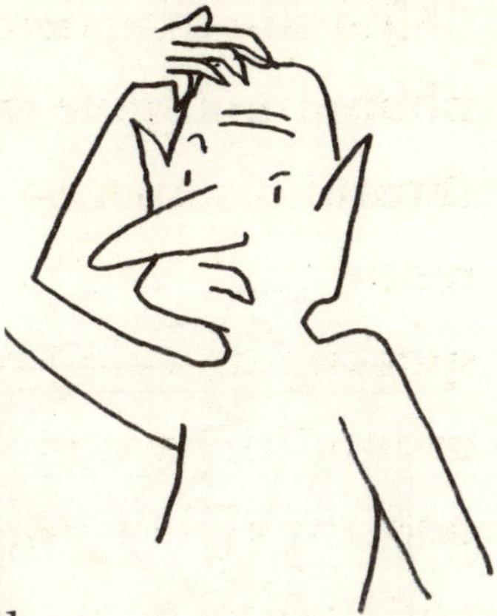

"Thanks, Kirsty!"

The goblin looked as if he couldn't quite believe what had just happened. "But..." he stuttered. "But..." He stamped his foot. "You tricked me!" he yelled.

Rachel shook her head. "Tasha won that ribbon fairly when she danced better than you," she told him. "But you wouldn't give it to her. So what choice did we have?"

The goblin glared. "Thieves! Cheats!" he fumed. "Tricksters!"

Tasha looked stern. "Jack Frost shouldn't have taken the ribbons in the first place," she reminded him.

"He's the thief, not us!"

"And you're a thief, too," Kirsty said, "stealing someone else's tap shoes and cane like that!"

The goblin stuck his tongue out. "Well, you're not getting the *shoes* back," he said, glancing down at them. "I'm keeping them to dance with." And as if to prove it, he started dancing. However, without the ribbon's magical powers, he had no sense of rhythm *or* balance and moments later, he tripped over and landed on his bottom.

His face flushed dark green with rage and he took off the shoes and hurled them into the corner of the room.

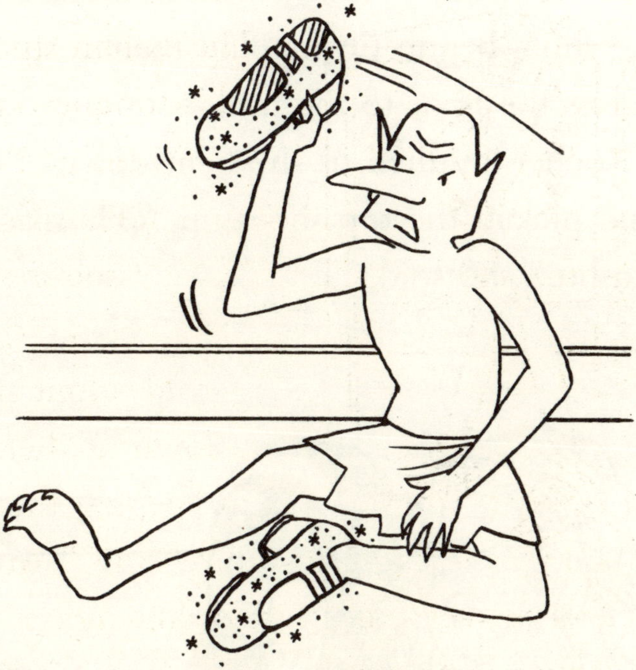

"Stupid shoes!" he muttered, then jumped to his feet and stomped off in disgust.

Tasha pointed her wand at the shoes. A stream of fairy dust and little top hats swirled from the tip of her wand and floated gently over to them. Immediately the shoes began tip-tapping their way across the floor to the girls.

Rachel laughed as she bent down and picked the tap shoes up. "Thanks, Tasha," she said.

"I should be thanking you two," Tasha replied. "You've both been wonderful, but now I must return to Fairyland! Goodbye, girls." And blowing kisses to Rachel and Kirsty, Tasha disappeared in a shower of ruby red sparkles.

Rachel and Kirsty waved goodbye and then went to look for Ashleigh.

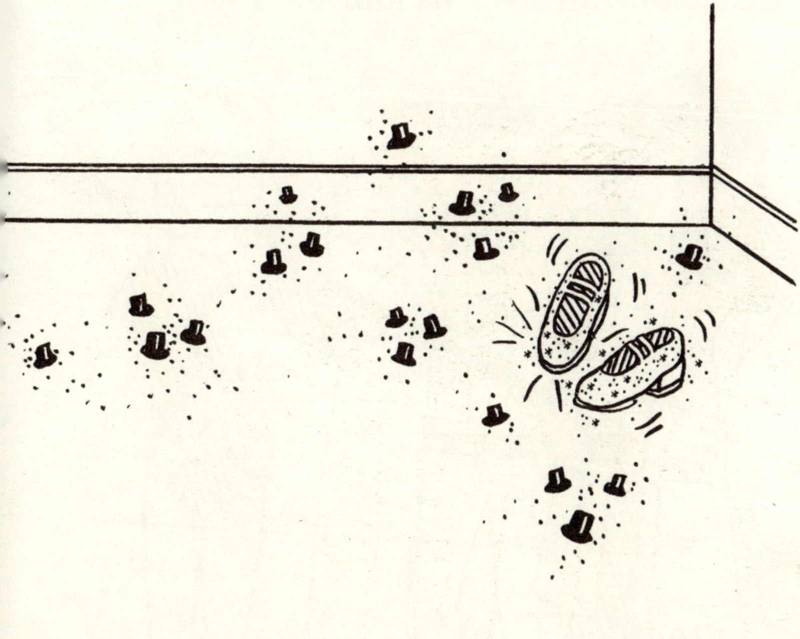

"Oh, thank you!" Ashleigh beamed, when she saw her shoes and cane. "You've saved the day! We're just about to start our show."

"You're welcome," Rachel said, smiling.

"We're looking forward to seeing you dance," Kirsty added.

Rachel and Kirsty watched as Ashleigh ran over to join the rest

of her dance class, ready for their performance. The teacher introduced the dance and turned on the music.

Rachel and Kirsty couldn't help feeling a tiny bit nervous as they watched – they'd seen so many dance performances go wrong lately! But this one went perfectly and Ashleigh's dancing was beautiful.

"And it's all because Tasha's got her ribbon back again," Kirsty said happily.

"Yes," Rachel agreed with a grin. "I love helping the fairies!"

Dazzling Dance Fairies part 2

Don't miss out on what happens next,
and make sure you read the
Dazzling Dance Fairies Collection 2!

Now it's time for Rachel and Kirsty to help

Jessica the Jazz Fairy

Read on for a sneak peek...

"I'm so-o-o excited!" Kirsty Tate said happily, smoothing down the satiny skirt of her long purple dress. "I've never been to a really *grown-up* party before!"

"Me neither," Rachel Walker, Kirsty's best friend, agreed. Like Kirsty, she was dressed in one of her favourite outfits, a floaty ivory-coloured dress with sequins around the hem and neckline. Along with Kirsty's parents, the girls were on their way to a party at the home of Alexander Willow, who was a friend of Mr and Mrs Tate's.

"It's not far now," Mr Tate replied, steering the car down the narrow, dark country lane. "You're going to have a great time, girls. Alexander's a producer of West End musicals, and he always throws *grown-up* parties!"

"Yes, there's going to be a jazz band and lots of dancing!" added Mrs Tate.

In the back of the car, Kirsty and Rachel exchanged an anxious glance.

While Rachel was staying with Kirsty over the half-term holiday, the two girls had been helping their very special friends, the Dance Fairies, find their missing magic Dance Ribbons. The ribbons were very important because their magic made sure that all kinds of dancing were fun, in both Fairyland and the human world, and also that dance performances went well. Jack Frost had stolen the ribbons for himself because he wanted their magic powers to help his goblins learn to dance.

When the King and Queen of Fairyland had demanded that the ribbons be returned to the Dance Fairies, Jack Frost's icy spell had sent seven of his goblin servants tumbling away into the human world, each goblin clutching one of the magic ribbons. The goblins were supposed to keep the ribbons hidden, but so far Kirsty and Rachel, with the help of the Dance Fairies, had managed to get four of them back.

"Jessica the Jazz Fairy's ribbon is still missing," Kirsty whispered eagerly.

"Maybe the goblin who has her ribbon will be at the party tonight!"

Rachel nodded. The girls knew that the magical ribbon was attracted to its own type of dance. "I hope so too, Kirsty," Rachel whispered. "We must get the ribbon back otherwise the party will be ruined!"

"What kind of dancing will there be, Mum?" Kirsty asked as Mr Tate drove between two wrought iron gates and up a long, winding driveway. "Rachel and I don't really know what jazz dance is!"

Mrs Tate nodded. "Jazz music is quite modern, and so is jazz dance," she explained. "In fact, you've probably both seen lots of jazz dancing in musicals."

"Oh, great!" Rachel exclaimed happily, "I *love* that kind of dancing!"

Kirsty was peering out of the car window, her eyes wide. "I've never seen such an *enormous* garden!" she said. "Rachel, look at that pond with the mermaid fountain in the middle."

Rachel looked out of the window. "And at the house!" she added, pointing.

The manor house in front of them was huge and very impressive with lots of windows and a large wooden door that stood ajar, flanked by flaming torches. Rows of cars were already parked outside, and people were climbing out of them. The women were dressed in long, elegant ballgowns in a rainbow of colours and the men all wore smart suits.

As they entered the hall of the manor house, the girls looked around eagerly. The house was lit by tall, pillar-shaped white candles whose flickering flames filled the hall with a warm yellow glow. Golden chocolate coins had been scattered over the antique tables and large gold platters piled high with bejewelled cupcakes had been placed here and there.

"Oh, this is *gorgeous!*" Kirsty sighed.

Everyone else was making their way through the house towards the back garden, so the Tates and Rachel followed.

The garden was even more spectacular than the house. Kirsty and Rachel stared open-mouthed as they walked past exotic plants in huge china pots, a rippling aquamarine swimming pool and an intricate maze constructed of neatly-clipped hedges.

A white marquee had been erected in the middle of the garden for the party. As the girls walked in, they could see that gold sparkling stars decorated the roof of the marquee, and tables and chairs had been set up for the guests. A jazz band sat on a platform at the back, playing a catchy tune that quickly had Kirsty and Rachel tapping their toes.

"Nobody's dancing yet, thank goodness!" Rachel whispered, noting the empty dance floor in the middle of the marquee.

"Everyone's too busy eating and talking," Kirsty whispered back, watching the waiters who were carrying around trays of drinks and offering them to the guests. "But there are lots of places for a goblin to hide!"

Rachel nodded. "We'll just have to keep looking," she said determinedly, scanning the marquee.

"That's Alexander over there, girls," said Mrs Tate, pointing to a tall, fair-haired man who was chatting with other guests. "We'll introduce you later, but I can tell you're longing to explore. Why don't you go and have a look around now?"

"Thanks, Mum," Kirsty said. And she and Rachel wandered off, winding their way between the chairs and tables.

"Would you like a fruit juice cocktail, girls?" asked a waiter. He was holding a tray on which stood two tall crystal glasses decorated with pretty paper umbrellas.
"They're delicious."

"Yes, please!" Kirsty and Rachel chorused, each taking one of the glasses.

Rachel took a sip. "Yum!" she exclaimed as the waiter hurried off. "It's delicious!"

Kirsty raised the glass to her lips to take a sip herself. But then she gasped aloud, because, there, sitting on the rim of the crystal glass, twirling the umbrella and smiling up at her, was Jessica the Jazz Fairy.

"Rachel, look!" Kirsty laughed as Jessica rose to her feet, still holding the umbrella. Balancing daintily on the edge of the glass, the tiny fairy waved up at the girls. She wore a silky pink dress with a deeper pink sash and a matching long, pink feather boa around her neck. High-heeled silver shoes sparkled on her feet, and golden curls tumbled down her back.

"Hello, girls," Jessica called softly, putting down the umbrella. "I've come to find my ribbon!"

Quickly Kirsty and Rachel hurried over to a quiet corner of the marquee away from the other guests. Jessica took a cautious look around and then fluttered from the glass onto Kirsty's shoulder.

"Is your ribbon here, Jessica?" Rachel asked eagerly.

Jessica nodded. "I'm sure it is!" she replied. "The magic of my ribbon will have brought the goblin here because the party has a jazz theme!"

"Ladies and gentlemen!" came a loud announcement from the stage, making Rachel and Kirsty jump.

The girls turned to see what was

going on. The saxophone player from the jazz band had stepped up to the microphone and was beaming at the audience.

"As a special birthday present for Alexander, the cast of his new musical, *Jazz It Up!* are going to perform a number from the show just for him!" the musician explained.

The guests broke into applause and cheers, and Alexander Willow looked surprised but very pleased.

"Oh, this is going to be a disaster without Jessica's magic ribbon!" Rachel said anxiously, as the dancers ran onto the stage to more applause. They looked very stylish. The women were dressed in short sequinned skirts and waistcoats while the men wore black trousers, white shirts and silk scarves knotted around their necks. They all had sparkling top hats on their heads.

Jessica was looking very sad.

"This would be a *fabulous* performance if only the Jazz Ribbon was in its proper place on my wand!" she sighed.

The jazz band struck up an upbeat tune as the dancers quickly took their places. They began to shimmy across the stage, throwing their arms up into the air in sequence, and singing,

Jazz it up!
Join us tonight and Jazz it up!

Meet the Sweet Fairies

Also available as an ebook

If Kirsty and Rachel don't find
the Sweet Fairies' magical charms,
Jack Frost will ruin all sweet treats for ever!

www.rainbowmagicbooks.co.uk

Win Rainbow Magic Goodies!

There are lots of Rainbow Magic fairies, and we want to know which one is your favourite! Send us a picture of her and tell us in thirty words why she is your favourite and why you like Rainbow Magic books. Each month we will put the entries into a draw and select one winner to receive a Rainbow Magic Sparkly T-shirt and Goody Bag!

Send your entry on a postcard to Rainbow Magic Competition,
Orchard Books, 338 Euston Road, London NW1 3BH.
Australian readers should email: childrens.books@hachette.com.au
New Zealand readers should write to Rainbow Magic Competition,
4 Whetu Place, Mairangi Bay, Auckland NZ.
Don't forget to include your name and address.
Only one entry per child.

Good luck!